Bettina Warzecha

The Problem with Quality Management

Process orientation, controllability and
zero-defect processes as modern myths

Translated into English by Swintha Danielsen

Philosophy in Practice 1

Verlag für Planung und Organisation 2017

Original title: *Problem: Qualitätsmanagement*, Walsrode 2009

Copyright © 2017 Bettina Warzecha

Publisher: Verlag für Planung und Organisation, Walsrode, Germany, verlag.planungundorganisation@t-online.de.

Production: Books on Demand GmbH, Norderstedt, Germany.

Cover design: Andrea Keßler (www.kessler-creativdesign.de)

Additional graphics: Heinz W. Pahlke

Proof reader of the English translations: Robert Kinsella (The Language Boutique, Düsseldorf)

Warzecha, Bettina. 2017. *The Problem with Quality Management: Process orientation, controllability and zero-defect processes as modern myths*. Philosophy in Practice 1. Walsrode, Germany: Verlag für Planung und Organisation.

ISBN 978-3-9818638-0-2

Preface

Quality management (QM) is the name of one of the most important procedures with which organizations are supposed to be led and managed. In companies, administrations, schools and universities, hospitals and charity organizations – all are looking for possible "standards" that are discussed and approved in working group meetings and committees.

Many of those involved in QM follow the conviction that with its help the quality of products and services can be "continuously improved". QM seems to be closely related to the approved measures and testing techniques with which high quality goods of all kinds are proven. Who would not be a friend of the improvement of the quality in management?

However, this overlooks the fact that QM does not have much in common with the measurements of product quality – and even less with improvement in a general sense. The word "quality" is supposed to counter possible obstacles, as the fathers of QM affirm generously. As is well known, good bait catches fine fish.

Table of contents

List of Tables

List of Images

I. What is quality and what is the subject of quality management (QM)?

1. The general word "quality"

Quality generally stands for the good, for what everybody desires, for the unquestionable, for sense and reason. Quality appears like a value by itself, which does not need to be justified further.

Unfortunately, nonetheless, what is often the case with the "good": not everyone is fascinated by it. For some people what the neighbour regards as quality is a dread. Just take a walk through a new housing area and have a look at a Scandinavian style house that has been built on the basis of 3-litre, energy-saving dwelling, right next to a futuristic designer house with all sorts of luxuries. Both home-owners will be intrigued by the quality they have managed to afford. And still, apart from this similarity, they do not seem to have much in common.

Quality is always both. It is something relative and subjective, which changes with the individual perspective. Nonetheless, it cannot be denied that people can well distinguish between good and bad, between right and wrong. Unquestionable, "objective" quality criteria for technical products are, for instance, functionality, durability, environment friendliness, user and restoration friendliness. Food is generally of good quality if it has all necessary nutrients, minerals and vitamins, and is not contaminated.

The ambiguity of the word quality can be traced back to a paradox, which will be examined further by taking a closer look at two quality criteria of clothing: fashionable and warming. However, in order to define these two characteristics, we have to bear in mind the basic rules of definition: the word to be defined cannot be part of the explanation. Thus, the quality criteria "fashionable" and "warming" have to be described without using these same words.

What is "fashion"? The definition in German Brockhaus states: "A style of an epoch that changes quickly with changing preferences of a culture, civilization or lifestyle. Fashion is produced on a short-term basis, is not predictable and arbitrary."[1] But what is a "preference", "culture", or "civilization"? Moreover, the definition of these words makes their relationship to other words necessary, which again need to be explained. The attempt to define what is "fashionable" thus does not end at all. The assignment of the quality criterion "fashionable" to a piece of clothing depends on numerous criteria (upon which two competing designers could never agree). The description of the criterion "fashionable" leads us to infinity, into a so-called "infinite regress". It is possible to say something about this criterion, but it is still impossible to capture it with certainty.

Now perhaps the quality criterion "warming" can be described better. The property "warming" means that a particular body temperature is maintained. What is "temperature"? Temperature is measured according to the expansion of particular substances. What is "expansion"? Expansion is not only the main feature of the room (this aspect can be safely neglected here), but the change in temperature by heat (heating). What causes the change in body temperature by heating? Now the word cannot be avoided any longer: it is warmth! We have now thought in a circle – in a vicious circle (Mauthner 1923: 248-250). Such a circle is right, but it also lacks explanation. In this case it means: warmth = warmth. The quality criterion "warming" is met if the piece of clothes provides warmth.

The problem of any definition of "quality" is therefore the fact that a single quality criterion can only be defined with its

---

[1] Note that the German word *Mode* "fashion" does not have a similarly broad meaning as the English translation. For our purpose, please ignore the other meanings of the word in English.

surroundings – namely the whole. The danger of getting lost in this whole (in an infinite regress) is then just as big as the danger of ending up with circular argumentation (in a vicious circle).

Nonetheless, the paradox of the meaning of quality has never been a reason for giving up the search for real quality in times prior to quality management. In relation to traditional discourses in philosophy, it was said that quality is the real good and right. Even though this is not captured or described well by language, quality would be realized in the experience of the senses and the use. Real quality includes values that are independent of culture and time, values that concern all people.

2. The "quality" in quality management (QM)

The requirements of "quality" which are generally presupposed without question are not even met in part by QM. Usually there is silence with respect to any concrete definition. In QM insider circles nowadays – if a definition cannot be completely avoided – they refer at best to a definition after which quality is present if the requirements proposed beforehand are met in a production process. According to this interpretation, quality criteria are proposed and demanded by the decision makers in an organization. The management demands the requirements – and if these are met, this is quality. Table 1 contrasts the general understanding (common sense) of quality to the one in QM.

While the general concept of quality is oriented to traditional values, the QM quality concept seems completely devoid of content. The extensive explanations and notes that often accompany this term support the impression that something is defined that in fact remains completely in the dark. The barely existing semantic content of the concise definition of quality does not become clearer with these notes, but rather once again it is relativized and appeased away. At the end

Quality in common sense	Quality in QM
Quality is the goodness or the value of a product. Value here: *excellence*, which can only be perceived with *experience*.	Quality is the degree to which the earlier demanded requirements are met. Value here: profit that is created if the product/service meets requirements with acceptable expenses.
Value is decisively determined by the use. Emphasized is the *usage value* (degree of usefulness, subjective value).	Value is decisively determined by the profit. Emphasized is the *exchange value* (market value, objective value).
Values determining the quality (use assignment) are rather independent of time and culture. A quality product should, e.g., be functional, durable and easy to operate and maintain.	Requirements (standards) that produce quality can be determined independent of general value concepts and relatively arbitrarily: "The first erroneous assumption is that quality means goodness, or luxury, ... we must define quality as 'conformance to requirements' if we are to manage it. If a Cadillac conforms to all the requirements of a Cadillac, then it is a quality car." (Crosby 1980)

Table 1: Comparison of the general understanding in the common sense of quality to the specific interpretation in QM

we get a ghostly, lifeless emptiness ready at all times to be filled with absurdities and stupidities of any kind.

While on the one hand in QM genuine quality can be reduced to any arbitrariness, there is also a "value" to be created. And this value can be measured, recounted unconditionally in large and in small amounts. The latest economic crisis is an indicator that such calculations at the expense of customers, employees and society – finally at the expense of businesses – can be done for some time. However, shortened quality logic is not only the trigger of the crisis. The firm anchoring of this logic in almost all areas of society – in quality managed schools and hospitals, in charity organizations and universities – is a good reason to move forward in this manner. In spite of quite obvious problems, questions for genuine quality and generally accepted values in products and services are considered as heresy of incorrigible idealists.

3. The procedures in quality management (QM)

In QM, "quality" has little to do with a general goodness or generally recognized values. The point is rather to make processes and products so that they comply with pre-established objectives and criteria. Here, QM essentially follows the steps of classical corporate planning. However, the difference to conventional planning is the claim to absoluteness in QM. This refers not only to the planning issues (as far as possible everything), the planning time (immediately and at the same time) and the degree of resolution of the planning (highly differentiated), but also to the accuracy (and without error) and steerability of the results (processes should be controllable).

Will these goals of omnipotence ever be accomplished? Historical development shows that their pursuit has always ended tragically. In any organization the dimensions of an exuberant complexity display in their own way. Planning includes the design and order of a myriad of different steps and the coordination of these steps with each other. QM seeks to master complexity by an equally complex planning process: through the meticulous dissection of the organizational action in detectable items, through continuous controlled processes and through the tireless gathering of records. Hence, in QM we are always busy with recounting thoroughly how much time employees need for single tasks, how often customers complain, how many tasks students could solve in comparative tests, etc. Anyone who complains about such calculation procedures is taught by the quality managers that we can only improve later what can be measured before and afterwards.

When everything is finally collected and counted that seems suitable for this purpose, then another planning step is the handling of the investigated processes in new ways. In conventional planning, this step involves mainly the optimization of the given procedures. In QM one strives by far higher in this planning phase: controlled processes and zero-error qualities seem to be possible only due to the given abundance of collected data.

Taking into account the fact that QM is less about technical and rather more about social processes – namely processes of managing – such claims are astonishing. Each organization scientist knows that in social processes not too much can be dominated and often only the non-essential can be measured. Even if all the tangible processes in the form of countless differentiated documents – just like a real golden calf of multiplicity – can be combined to form a remarkable construct, this usually does not contain much truth. The smallest process parts that are there in the tombs of data cemeteries are less about truth but are instead the sad end of a QM division.

Torn contexts of meaning are the result of modern belief that complexity can be controlled by complexity. A real "improvement" through planning is much more than the mere finding of compliance with requirements. The zealous attempt to make improvements visible in measurements is something other than improvement itself. You can thus learn without measuring/testing all the new knowledge. Products can achieve a higher quality level by using better raw materials and by better processing, which is not accessible to the existing measuring instruments. Merely the reduction to the essentials opens countless opportunities for improvement of products and services.

In the pages that follow, various aspects of QM are considered in more detail. It will become clear in what way QM sacrifices quality, knowledge, motivation, ingenuity, material and financial resources and – last but not least – values and morals.

II. The myth of "process orientation"

1. The process problem I: Processes and structures are two sides of the same coin

In QM, it is a common strategy to equate processes with change, movement, progress and speed, while structures are taken as a standstill and inflexibility. There is no doubt that quality movement orients itself on processes. In a quality management organization, dynamic processes are finally supposed to control the frozen structures. However, a closer look reveals that processes and structures are bound so tightly that their distinction is a very artificial endeavour.

Let us take a look at Image 1, one of the most famous pictures by the artist M.C. Escher. We believe to know at first sight what is in motion in this picture: flying birds. We arrive at this judgement due to earlier experience, with the help of which we categorize and interpret new information. We know what a bird looks like. And we know what it looks like when birds fly. When looking at Image 1, we thus compare the structures of the picture with a structure that has already been saved in our memories.

Let us now have a closer look at the picture. What kind of birds are these? Where are they flying? At what time of day does this flight take place? For the observer it is impossible to answer these questions. Is the picture about white birds flying through the night from left to right? Or are we dealing with black birds moving at daylight from right to left? No matter how long we look at the picture, we will not be able to determine the answers.

There is only one possibility of answering these questions with any certainty: We have to take the picture as in motion. Through motion it can be decided what is moving (white or black birds), how they are moving (from left to right or the other way around), and when this is happening (at night or in daytime). Structures can thus be perceived in movement. Through motion – meaning through processes – the structures, being the distinct and constant units, become apparent.

Image 1: Day and night, by M.C. Escher[2]

And conversely it is also true that only through unchangeable structures and through distinct units can movement and change (i.e. processes) be perceived. The perception of processes implies the simultaneous existence of constant things, such as structures. Without structure, we would not get an idea of movement or processes in Image 1.[3]

---

[2] Acknowledgement: M.C. Escher's "Day and Night", © 2017 The M.C. Escher Company - The Netherlands. All rights reserved. www.mcescher.com

[3] Likewise, the description of processes in metabolism implies that structures (people, animals, plants, sky and earth) exist, which can be distinguished from each other – at least for a certain time. The artificiality of such structures, represented through every little metabolism process, through every breath, has been described differently, depending on the religious and culture-historical backgrounds. These distinctions in descriptions hint at the illusion of distinctness of structure and processes. In physics, the relativity principle shows that movements (processes) are only describable relative to other movements (processes). And accordingly, it is only a question of the illusionary habit, when supposing that an object is in a state of rest (as a "structure"). The blindspot of this relativist view is enlightened e.g. by Aristotle with his concept of absolute silence or in Buddhism with its concept of emptiness. These explanations could also provide us with a solution to the riddle of motion and standstill, of processes

As has been so well visualized in the picture by Escher (Image 1), structure and process are two sides of the same coin. If in QM the process-oriented view is preferred to the structure-oriented view, then in fact, neither structures nor processes have lost any of their significance. Every process is the outcome of structures and again creates structures of its own in the end.[4]

If, for instance, a work group is formed as a quality circle with the goal of overhauling the production process completely, then its members often have a large creative leeway. The head of the team will express this in comments like the following: "Imagine you were starting from scratch. Forget the old procedures. In the coming days, you have all creative freedom. Think the unthinkable!" Who does not believe that when everything is set into motion that ultimately the processes dominate the frozen structures?

Nonetheless, every participant of such a circle knows how this new start finally ends in meeting rooms with their walls full of metaplan wallpaper and flip chart sheets. Even if the unthinkable is being thought, the power of the factual and already existing situation, the prevailing former structures will prevent radical changes. And also those changes

---

and structures, namely by the ignorance of any movement whatsoever. Scholars of all religions and the most significant philosophers take this silent emptiness as the real, unchanging state of all being, and not a moving, deterministic, or even chaotic processing. At this point we cannot decide if in fact the stillness is a form of movement (structure expressing processes), or if movement is a particular form of stillness (processes expressing structure, compare also footnote 7).

[4] In addition, the so-called *recursion* describes the paradox of the indistinguishable character of structures and processes. Linguistic and mathematical argumentation systems (or theories based upon them) generally return to their starting point in such a self-referential system, presupposing their argumentation is "right". This loop-like motion creates fixed structures, which only get recognizable through repetition and recursion. This problem of circular self-reference is best illustrated in every good dictionary, where we also find expressions being described through other expressions, which are again described through expressions that are, etc. (cf. chapter III, section 3 in this respect or e.g. Hofstadter (1999).

proposed by such a quality circle will again evolve into tight structures in the process of implementation – that is, into requirements that have to be fulfilled.

The rhetorical emphasis of processes in QM obscures and ignores the sight on the structures that stand behind and before them. This ignorance is truly dangerous for an organization and can ultimately prevent every further progress. This was an extensive subject in the 1980s in Organization Theory, and it is considered here in chapter III.

2. The process problem II: Process/divisional organization against functional organization – a sham battle

Companies and administrations can be organized – namely structured – in different ways. The structure of an organization is readable from the so-called "organigram". All processes, all action flows and events orient themselves towards these structural specifications. A traditional way of organizing is *functional organization*, sketched in Image 2 in a simplified manner.

The decision-making processes from top to bottom are here determined extensively through the hierarchical facts, while the horizontal decision-making processes, thus from left to right, have to be coordinated between the departments. In QM, this model is assumed to be hopelessly out of date. Solely those companies can clutch to this structure of functional organization that always produce the same products in the same procedure for the same supposed clients. This means those companies that lack real (dynamic!) challenges in their uniformity.

Therefore, functional organization is opposed by *process/divisional organization* (cf. Image 3). In this system, the authoritative decision-making processes proceed in a functional organization turned around by 90°.

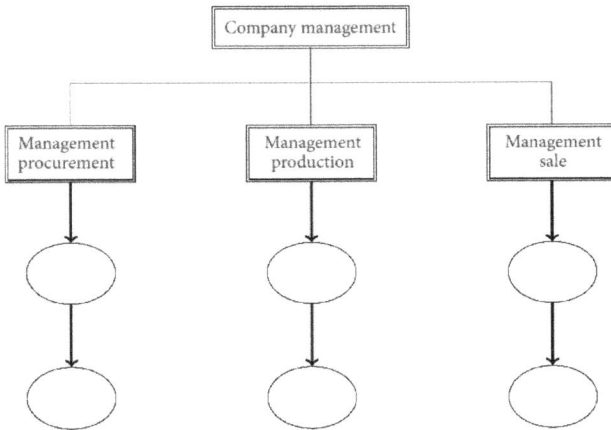

Image 2: Direction of processes in functional organization

The decision-making structures are no longer determined vertically, but rather horizontally. Process or product managers replace the earlier department managers under their responsibility. The problematic interfaces thus no longer exist between the departments, but rather between the responsibility areas of the respective process managers. In this kind of organization structure, negotiation processes between the process managers work vertically. This possibly involves the (former) department managers, who may then have some staff position within process/divisional organization at best.

The profit of such a reversal remains however in the dark. In the so-called "process/divisional organization", processes obviously do not have any other, let alone "more" significance than in the functional organization. It is argued here that in

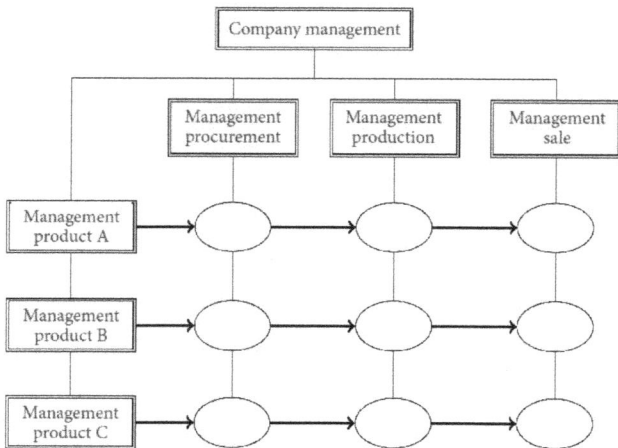

Image 3: Direction of processes in process/divisional organization

QM the important processes in an organization would not take place within the departments, but rather horizontally through the departments. The organigram of an organization should therefore always be viewed from left to right. This is almost as if asking the admirer of a painting to look at it from left to right rather than from top to bottom, in order to see the most relevant features. Even more bizarre in QM is the frequently uttered assumption that the horizontal organization operations may well be processes, but the vertical department procedures are not.

The problem of the structural firmness of decision processes in organizations remains the same: Irrelevant of how the determinations take place – the naming of the decision makers also decides who shall not decide. The competence of those, however, is sometimes even more relevant. In order to solve this problem in QM, it is suggested that functional organization should not be replaced by process/divisional organization, but to only add the process or product managers on the horizontal level.

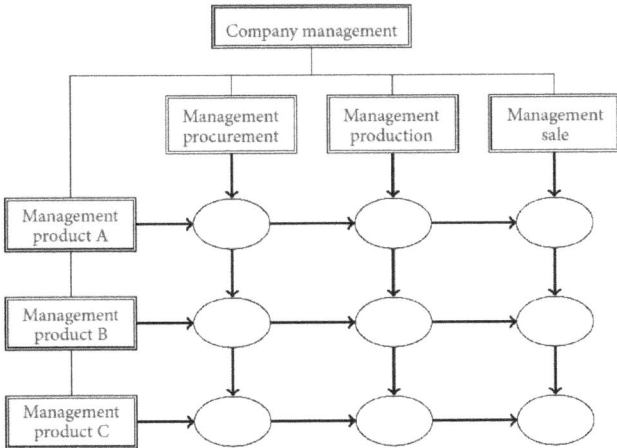

Image 4: Direction of processes in matrix organization

Applying such a dual organization form, which is also called matrix organization (cf. Image 4) means that the decision processes would happen as in the following example:

> *The manager of a mobile phone company regards the sales problem to be the result of mistakes in the product's development. However, the person responsible for the process, the product manager, finds failures in the marketing. In the production division,*

they have realized that a problem with the delivery of vendor parts restricts the user friendliness. Up to that, the controller, who is responsible for bench marketing noticed that the mobile phones are not in line with market prices. He suggests that a reduction of the prices would be indispensable for a stimulation of the sale.

Now what to do? Shall we be "process-oriented" and prefer the suggestions made by the process or product manager from the "better horizontal" perspective over other perspectives? However on the basis of which arguments? In the dual organization, decisions could be made either by the product manager, the responsible of the production division, or by the company manager and the controller. This facilitates the greatest possible change (horizontally, vertically, centrally...), yes, an almost "multidimensional processing". Everything could be decided and resolved "just in time", spontaneously and in one stroke. Then, in our example, with the help of a greater advertisement expenditure, we would have mobile phones that are produced more costly but also more user-friendly and end up cheaper on the market. At the very end of this process chain our mobile phone producer would probably be declared unavoidably bankrupt, under dual process/divisional organization.

This example demonstrates that it is not possible to follow various directions of decisions and at the same time reduce the problem of decision-making processes. The problems look different from above than from below, and also different from the centre than from the sides. Negotiation processes do not get simpler if the number of decision-makers rises, as it is the case with the instituting of the process or product managers. They do not improve if the decision-making structures happen completely horizontally instead of vertically. The problem described here is not new. It has always been known in Organization Theory from the experiences of functional organization with project teams, with staff positions and staff divisions. There they also have the goal to work on the questions that cannot be dealt with completely in the departments. The label "process/divisional organization" obscures the view on such already made experiences, as well as on such solutions of decision-making in organizations that are worth mentioning.

3. The process problem III: More and more interfaces

The term *interface*, which is originally taken from natural sciences, tries to describe the borderline between two systems. This borderline, however, is constructed in a paradoxical way. On the one hand, it is not passable, because every system can only operate or act with reference to itself, and thus they are a "black box" for other systems (Luhmann 1984: 593f.).[5] On the other hand, communication becomes possible where the respective surfaces coincide precisely.

This technical description of interfaces can also be transferred to social processes, in which the interface person/person is observed. It can be argued that here every psychological system (every person) only operates (i.e. thinks, decides and acts) in a self-referring manner. System crossing contacts are not directly possible. You can tell somebody your thoughts, but you cannot insert them directly into his or her thinking activities. Therefore, the term *interface* does not only refer to the simple borderline that can be crossed with the right instruments. It also refers to the problem of the unavoidable final friction loss, which happens due to the different ways of operation of the distinct systems.

---

[5] The "black box" is an object, whose inner constitution and inner work processes are not known.

In the physical-technical area, the friction loss can be easily identified. In social processes they are expressed through knowledge, information and coordination problems – and not least, in power struggles. In the social area, the actors are in fact a "black box", which will also stay incalculable in future.

QM likes to promise that the change from functional organization to process/divisional organization can reduce the interface problem co-worker/co-workers. The co-workers would then block less, because the now mobilized processes break the frozen structures. However, we have seen in the preceding section that, in so-called "process/divisional organization", processes do not proceed differently than in functional organization. And in spite of all labelling, also the problem of structural determination is not minimized in QM. Quite to the contrary! Already the additionally introduced positions for process or product managers determine further structures. And these structures cause the further freezing of decision-making circumstances. As will be explained in the next section, this problem is also empowered via QM due to the fact that work processes are determined in smaller and smaller steps and thus become more differentiated. Thus, in QM, an organization is pared down in ever-smaller units with more and more interfaces.

Let's take, for example, the often discredited interface in planning of social services: There are, on the one hand, the social workers, who are supposed to improve the psychological situation of the clients. On the other, there are the officials in charge, who are mainly responsible for the financial support of the clients. The scope of action of both groups of employees is increasingly differentiated through the increasingly precise regulatory requirements. But not everything can be determined. Especially the clients and their social problems are rarely ever categorizable due to the requirements. And this means that decision processes at the interface of the social workers and the administration would be a necessary precondition for valuable help. In fact, the given structures determined in QM processes in an increasingly differentiated way are set as the "rock solid" standards and make real negotiation impossible. This not only demeans the competence of both groups of professionals but also the human dignity of the clients. Their right to get support is nowadays not only reduced by single principle riders, but also by a whole cavalry of standards.

It cannot be expected that the unity and the collaboration of different units of an organization improve with more dissected requirements of work and decision-making structures. How can we then explain the QM fantasy that the creation of ever-increasing interfaces will solve the problem of interfaces? We can only speculate on that. Maybe it is the inevitable creation of complexity in the end, which appears chaotic to the involved persons. And this provokes the hallucinogenic impression that now all structures/interfaces are really mobilized.

4. The process problem IV: The loss of holism

In the preceding sections, we have shown that the so-called "process orientation" in QM does not result in any new treatment of processes and structures. Likewise, the change from the so-called "functional" – meaning structure oriented – organization form to a "process/divisional organization" only induces the change in direction, in which everything that happens in an organization is viewed. At the same time, the problem of interfaces in social processes as in QM will be rather amplified than reduced. However, the term "process orientation" nowadays also refers to something else, which will be dis-cussed in detail, due to its relevance.

4.1. "Processing" means differentiating more and more in QM[6]

Every action is understood as a process under the norms and standards of QM. Each process should be recorded in a professional manner so that it is finally documentable in the form of ratios. Every event in an organization is thus to be registered highly differentiated. The goal of such an all-round documentation is the complete control of all organization processes through the management and the also complete control of the management itself.

In the implementation instructions of process orientation, it is often noted that the demanded documentation simply has to be according to the requirements. It is even claimed that after a phase of re-orientation, the documentation will use less paper, or less store capacity than before. However, in general, the already existing documentation will form the poor starting positions of process descriptions, and this is because we have to take into consideration all criteria that are explicated in the QM models. The final goal is the systematic, clearly structured and effective recording, analysis, and planning of

---

[6] "Differentiate" means "to notice a difference", a distinction, to make a division. Differentiation is for one the opposite of "uniting", and two, it is not explainable without reference to a superordinate unit. The literature expresses this paradox, e.g., with the pairs "difference and unit", "distinction and similarity", "part and whole", or also "element and system". The paradox already became apparent in antiquity in Zenon's description of the relations of "the part and the whole", similarly, in Russell's "element and class" at the beginning of the last century. In modern philosophy, there are, e.g., Leibnitz, Fichte, Hegel, and Schelling, who picked up this paradoxical relationship. These philosophers regarded differentiation – or difference – as an illusion of the restricted human mind, which can only be resolved through a superordinate unit, an indivisible whole. Also, in the different system theories, we find descriptions of the interaction between "element and system" – such as by Radcliffe-Brown, Wiener, von Glasersfeld, and Luhmann – in an ever-repeating pattern. In particular, the late writings by Luhmann let the paradox of "difference and unity" not only come out clearly in its whole (as he puts it) "painfulness", but also in its salutary indistinguishability.

all process aspects. The information that is necessary and has to be analysed for this, does not only refer to the process achievements and their conjunction with other elements of the processes. In the analysis we also have to include information about needs, expectations, and experiences of all interest groups. This means, we have to consider the clients, property owners, shareholders, employees, suppliers, and any other kind of company stakeholders. Thus, a good process description should take into account all possible and thinkable aspects and perspectives.

However, the right and comprehensive distinction, the right differentiation, is not only relevant for process planning. Also the process rules, which are the actual target of the planning, should be determined in a differentiated way. In order to obtain this, procedures that have so far only been communicated orally (or not at all) will be defined and written down bindingly. In QM, it is therefore mostly desired to extract the knowledge of the employees in the most differentiated manner and insert it into the formalized process descriptions. Implicit knowledge is to be made explicit. In the printed definitions, such as in the quality handbook, work processes are defined in an increasingly precise and therefore differentiated manner. The employees are obliged to fulfil these extremely differentiated requirements. Through this highly professional procedure, everything controllable should be controlled.

Table 2 illustrates the rough differentiation steps in a process description. These steps are expandable at will, and they can be combined in different variations with each other as well as once again be dispersed more precisely. With regard to the personnel descriptions, we can, for example, break down the need for training and the hierarchical conditions in several other differentiation steps. Work equipment and the necessary materials can be defined more precisely with respect to the predefined quality requirements by statutory requirements, customer needs, etc.

Process description	Process input	Process goals	Process ratios	Interfaces
Process step A	Designation of process officers Description of necessary qualification of the personnel Description of working materials Description of resources or sub-assemblies time frame, etc.	Goal 1 Goal 2 Goal 3 etc.	1. Ratio for goal 1, 2. Ratio for goal 1, 3. Ratio for goal 1. 1. Ratio for goal 2, etc.	Interfaces with other processes or process steps in companies
Process step B	See above (v.s.)	v.s.	v.s.	v.s.
Process step C	v.s.	v.s.	v.s.	v.s.
Process step D	v.s.	v.s.	v.s.	v.s.
Process step E	v.s.	v.s.	v.s.	v.s.

Table 2: A small selection of the differentiation steps in a process

Table 3 below contains criteria according to which the given processes are controlled, improved and redefined in the course. Again, any additions or further differentiations are conceivable. This arbitrary randomness is maxed out in practice. Thus, in the manuals of QM, there are, for instance, the criteria listed that explain how the definitions are to be defined, and thus they standardize how standards should be standardized.

Control and improvement// According to criteria	Correctness of the accomplish-ment	Compliance of the time frame	Reaching of goals	Occur-rence of mistakes
of the whole processes				
of the individual process steps				
of the interface descriptions				
of the purpose and goal of the process				
of the adequacy of the ratios				

Table 3: A small selection of control and improvement possibilities

4.2. The problematic nature of differentiation

If we want to get to the bottom of something, and if something quite unclear is to be examined, then differentiation has been an approved method. By means of differentiation we can divide one unclear whole into small manageable portions. It can be looked at from different (therefore differentiated) perspectives. At the end of such a differentiation process, there is generally new knowledge about the cause-effect relationships and new solutions appear. If process orientation in quality management is implemented primarily as differentiation, we build on this approved method of knowledge, a method that has proven to be very effective in mathematics and in the technical field. QM also assumes that wholes can be divided or differentiated into parts without any problem. But already in antiquity, philosophers have not only supported this assumption but also questioned it. All attempts to describe the relationship between part and whole as well as between difference and unity have ended in an irresolvable paradox. The problem of differentiation has traversed the history of philosophy for centuries, without seemingly having any big influence on the sciences and mathematics. Modern models of thinking have changed this fundamentally:

At the beginning of the 20th century, Bertrand Russell showed in the field of mathematics that the relationship between a set (a whole) with its elements (differences) can not simply be determined by fragmentation (cf. Sainsbury 2009: 168). Atom physics also presented its model of quantum mechanics, which tied in with the philosophical sceptics and actually confirmed them. While classical physics assumed that it were possible to disaggregate a whole into ever-smaller parts, quantum mechanics have shown that these supposed smallest parts could not be seized so easily.

Even worse: possibly these smallest parts did not even truly exist![7] Still, the physicists' despair is great with respect to this question. Thus their spectacular research enterprises also aim particularly at this question – enterprises often attended by of hundreds of physicists. The experiment to verify the so-called Higgs boson at least for the billionth part of a billionth of a second with physical measuring instruments

---

[7] Thus, Bohm & Hiley (1975, cited in Capra 2000: 138) conclude the following: "One is led to a new notion of unbroken wholeness which denies the classical idea of analyzability of the world into separately and independently existing parts... We have reversed the usual classical notion that the independent 'elementary parts' of the world are the fundamental reality, and that the various systems are merely particular contingent forms and arrangements of these parts. Rather, we say that inseparable quantum interconnectness of the whole universe is the fundamental reality, and that relatively independently behaving parts are merely particular and contingent forms within this whole."

can be interpreted as the gigantic attempt to capture the paradox itself.[8]

The problem of differentiation therefore always becomes particularly clear if after decades of repetition, the scientific knowledge derived from differentiated processes once again proves to be wrong. Even in the close framework of science, in which scientific laws have long been approved, the determination of cause-effect relationships is not without risk. The fallacies and debates in science listed in the following only represent a small sample of the big drama, which is performed daily anew.

A small sample of fallacies and debates from the history of science:

- The Earth is flat.
- The Earth is round.
- Nuclear energy is not dangerous.
- Energy-saving light bulbs are environmentally friendly.
- The climate does not change due to human action.
- Experiments of brain researchers will prove the existence or non-existence of the free will.
- Meteors made dinosaurs extinct.
- Providing hormones decreases the general risk of cancer in women.
- Cancer can be cured through early detection.

---

[8] In the research centre CERN near Geneva they created therefore a particle accelerator with the depth of 60 m and a weight of 10,000 tons. In this apparatus, the smallest particles are to be thrown to collide with the greatest possible force so that even smaller phenomena, like the Higgs boson, may be discovered. The physicists believe strongly that this Higgs boson would appear as a kind of final truth, or as Leon Ledermann, the Nobel price owner of physics once argued, as the "element of God". It is meant to lead the difference to the unity, the non-existence to the existence (to the "mass", as a physicist puts it).

- Identical twins are genetically identical.
- Natural constants – like the gravitation G, the velocity of light c, and the fine structure constant a – are always constant.

It is often supposed that if something works, also the differentiated explanations for this function are correct. However, there are often worlds between the explanation on the one hand and the actual process on the other. As an example, with the knowledge that the world is flat, navigation at sea was performed without a problem around the globe. And if (not only) in the Middle Ages a person was cured after a venesection or an exorcism, who wanted to prove that the cure was not achieved through – but in spite of – such tortures?

The problem of differentiation is not avoidable. In science, it can be limited by means of scientific surveys of new hypotheses in practice and through (self-referential) argumentations, with the help of which the new hypotheses are supported by the existing and approved knowledge. In QM, these possibilities to oppose the differentiation problem with an approved unity are not applied. As a matter of fact, generally the taken decisions are not tested in any scientific way. Nor are the QM commitments supported by the already existing scientific knowledge. The differentiation patterns in QM rather result from more or less arbitrary decision-finding processes (see chapter IV, section 2.4.).

4.3. What exactly happens during differentiation – in other words, the fragmentation of the whole in its parts?

Similar to the observation that the separation of "process and structure" is only a deception for the human mind, we notice that "difference and unity" are closely interwoven. In order to illustrate this, I first of all want to recount a well-known story:

In ancient times, a king came to a town where all the blind of the land lived. Among his entourage was also the powerful elephant, an animal that had formerly been unknown to the people of this town. Some more courageous inhabitants longed for the examination of this new being. They went to where they presumed the elephant to stand and grasped for the parts of the animal they could reach. They touched it and were surprised and finally went back to the other inhabitants of the town, who were already curious to hear their report.

The brave one who had managed to grasp the ear of the elephant said: "This animal is a large, flat and coarse carpet." The man who had stroked the tusks of the elephant was convinced: "This being is a plough-share." Each of them had felt another part of the elephant's body: "A giant column", "a thick tube", "a brush", "a large leaf of a tree", "a soft hollow body", "a snake"... In the end they debated who would now be right. Each one of them had only had contact with one part of the elephant. Nobody knew the whole elephant.

This problem occurs in every differentiation process. Nobody really knows the whole. Even though humans usually see with their eyes, their senses are nonetheless restricted. The perception of the world is after all a big noise, which may only be distorted by columns, hollow bodies, elephants and similar things from time to time. Images 5 and 6 are used to give an idea of the difference between an elephant and the carefully differentiated quality elephant.

In a similar fashion, the artwork by Ursus Wehrli illustrates the problem of differentiation. Wehrli dismantled the works of great painters in their parts and ordered them – meaning he re-assembled them according to prevailing notions of order and thoroughness (cf. Wehrli 2002). In his work, Picasso, like Kandinsky or Miró were differentiated (ordered) according to form, colour and size of single parts of the pictures. Again and again, we realize, like in the picture of the quality elephant, what can happen in such a differentiation process:

- The parts are cut out of their context.
- The outlines of the parts may have been cut at the wrong edges.
- Parts may be missing.
- Parts may be added.
- The size relationship of parts may change.
- Colours may be incorrectly reproduced.
- The new order does not make sense anymore.
- The new order makes a sense that is unrelated to the original picture, etc., etc.

If now the better understanding, the ordered view, exactly the analysis of the whole (of a photo, a piece of art, a text, a work process) is the aim and purpose of a fragmentation, then we are confronted with the same infinite error possibilities. In each differentiation process, there will also be errors made from these error possibilities. Every result of a differentiation process thus includes affirmations that are simply wrong in the original, former or latter perspective. And this is not only a problem for the differentiated analyses of arts critics.

How do we then erase errors in our modern understanding? Correct – through more careful differentiation. In our example, we could therefore depict the parts of the picture more precisely; measure the sizes and size relationships more exacting. The new order could be oriented more towards the original, etc.

If errors are unavoidable in a differentiation process, then we only produce more errors with more differentiations. The process of error production is repeated. In the process of

Image 5: The simple elephant (© Eric Isselée - www.Fotalia.com)

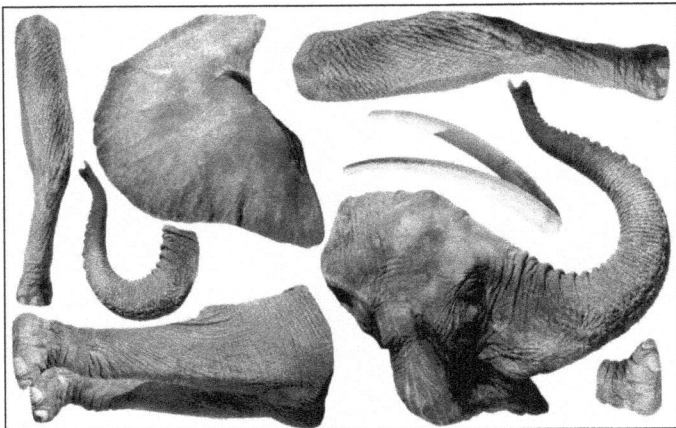

Image 6: The differentiated quality elephant

differentiation we thus want to erase errors by accepting ever more errors in the process. In arts, we may produce a new piece of art on its own accord by making more errors possible, as was shown by the works of Ursus Wehrli in an impressive way. In our day-to-day QM grind, it is, however, less expected that the processes and products become better with increasing errors of fragmentation.

4.4. The unavoidable consequences of steadily increasing dissection: Mistakes and manipulation possibilities rise abruptly

In the following, I present an incomplete list of errors – and hence also manipulation possibilities – that can occur in the framework of process orientation, being the differentiated examination of organizational processes:

Process elements are forgotten
- The most significant process feature is forgotten.
- Important facts are ignored.
- Less significant but for the whole process necessary features are missing.

Process elements are described wrongly
- Scientific knowledge is ignored.
- Scientific knowledge is integrated, but without being technically developed.
- Ratios do not measure what they pretend to (missing "validity").
- Ratios result from erroneous measuring (missing "reliability").

Process elements are evaluated incorrectly
- The emphasized significance proves to be trivial.
- The seemingly trivial is decisive for the process.

Process elements are put in wrong order
- The most significant is not done at the right moment.
- The less significant is done first.

Unnecessary process elements are added
- Process elements are added that can cause damage of, for instance, the product quality, the health of the employees or of the equipment.
- Process elements are added that produce unnecessary costs.

Process elements are separated or joined at the wrong places
- Connected parts of the process are separated.
- Process parts that should better be separate are connected.

Mutual dependencies of process elements are wrongly described
- The dependencies of process elements are derived from old knowledge.
- The dependencies of process elements are ignored.

The possibilities to insert errors into processes are surely infinite. Error possibilities can be expanded infinitely in companies, administrations and public institutions. These errors in an organization can not only refer to the description of employees' qualifications and actions, the consistency of the material, the end products and financial aspects. Errors are also possible with respect to taxes, law, ecology, marketing, work-related psychological and ethical aspects of any kind. What can go wrong will also eventually go wrong. In differentiation processes, it is not possible to ban errors.

And even the most probable seeming errors, such as the forgetting of the most significant process elements can be observed in practice. The employees of call centres, for example, are trained in politeness and the use of almost therapeutic appearing formulae for calming customers in order to improve customer satisfaction. This often overlooks the fact that these strategies were not even necessary if the most important – namely the competence – could be assured at the other end of the line.

For process orientation – that is the dissection of all work processes – the following holds: the more differentiated the requirements are, the more probable it is that the number of wrong interpretations, of miscalculations and misunderstandings increases. Moreover, this opens up various possibilities for manipulation of every kind. In a social field like QM, the given decision and power relationships manipulate the main contents of respective differentiation significantly.

4.5. About the deeper causes of error emergence in the processes of differentiation and dissection

In science, it was speculated a lot about the causes of errors that occur during the dissection of the whole into its parts. The source of the problem can be the fact that it is not possible to dissect a whole into parts in a meaningful way without referring to the whole as such. This problem is not only inherent in every dictionary. Even if in QM a meaningful dissection of processes should be described, then it is often forgotten that the knowledge about the whole process only makes this feasible.

An example can be found in the strategy planning of a company. In general, the process step "inventory" will be done before other process steps like problem analysis and the evaluation and determination of goals. However, the actual problem of every planning – the challenge of complexity – cannot be solved this way.

One possible solution to this problem that is applied in practice is the inclusion of concepts that are supposed to be elaborated upon in the further process steps already in the inventory. This means that, for instance, in the inventory of one area we do not survey the existing situation in a general and value-free way. Instead, only the components of the given situation that should be part of the following process steps, like the problem analysis and the evaluation are considered.

Many managers and planners consider the perfection of this method as a strategy close to reality and pragmatic. But here the snake bites its own tail. They plan what has been generally determined before. Thus, this example leads to the classical circular arguments and vicious circles in which the results are already determined by the input. False conclusions of this type are then a welcome opportunity for new planning projects.

Another frequent explanation of the errors in fragmentation processes is the fact that any fragmentation can only be done in a meaningful manner if we "compare" the dissection with earlier experience. Any dissection can only be thought in relation to another already existing dissection patterns that we have already saved in our memory.[9] Every process of thinking is a continuous comparing and relativization: A is better/ bigger/ prettier than B, which again is prettier/ worse/ more advantageous than C, whereas C is certainly only comparable with relation to D, which relates to E...

This model often used for thinking and fragmenting matches the processing of a computer, where constantly combinations of ones and zeros (power on, power off) are compared to other combinations of ones and zeros. If this process stops somewhere and at some point ceases to compare, then the computer crashes. A similar thing can happen if in the human thinking process XY is not compared any more with Z. Then there will always be someone who points at the problem of this standstill: "Here you have to differentiate much more!"

In the course of scientific progress we now have the situation that we differentiate – hence, dissecting wholes into their parts in all fields of the human existence. The number of

---

[9] This is similar to the measuring problem described in chapter IV, section 2.1: comparing is only possible in reference to other comparisons.

possibilities for comparison has thus been empowered with respect to the unknowing human being of the grey prehistory. We have therefore become smarter and smarter, as it seems. But every reader will see the dilemma: Enough is not enough. If our thinking only functions as a process of comparisons – and how else should it be explained – then every endpoint of this comparison process will be a great error. Only if we research forever (infinitely), we may in the end find the truth. In QM it is therefore argued: "There is nothing that cannot be improved – meaning, compared further."

This makes it more plausible that in particular the most talented ones keep on searching. And if the employees of quality managed hospitals, administrations and companies are only more concerned with this method of comparison, in order to find the best and right way, then patients, students, citizens and clients should appreciate these never-ending processes.

In particular, the doctors and nurses who are forced to use their time for increasingly complex methods of diagnosis and treatment in which they have to apply complicated documentation requirements and training in increasingly laborious accounting procedures cannot take care of patients.

And a teacher who nowadays needs more and more time for learning novel school pedagogical concepts, new programmes of support and demand as well as detailed students' evaluation forms should not be obstructed unnecessarily by the students. In the end it is the student – in particular in the view of school administrations fascinated by QM – who represents the unwanted endpoint and angle, clearly opposing the differentiating procedures fundamentally.

Finally, we should mention the manager that not only should have the ability to juggle over-dimensioned data collections, but who should also extend these collections to any size. The success of mainly the listed companies nowadays seems to be dependent only on the skilful manipulation of data. Clients, employees, and – as we often had to learn – also the investors are those points of danger in which such differentiation processes of management can crash unintentionally.

The problem in these examples is always the same: In infinite processes there may not be meaningful endpoints. Nothing is more dangerous than the obvious endpoints (in our examples the patients, the students, clients, employees or investors), where all comparison comes to a standstill. So in QM there always remains something that can possibly never be improved.

III. The myth of "zero-defect" quality

1. The cycle of continuous improvement

A basis of QM is the concept of "continuous improvement". For this purpose, everyone involved in a well-organized company is encouraged to learn constantly. The final goal of the continuous improvement should then be profitable innovation. Image 7 gives a simplified graphic representation of the basic features in the process of knowledge gaining.

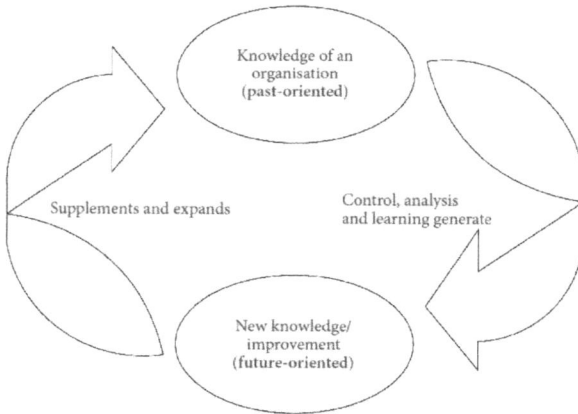

Knowledge of an organisation (past-oriented)

Control, analysis and learning generate

Supplements and expands

New knowledge/ improvement (future-oriented)

Image 7: The cycle of continuous improvement – improvement and given knowledge are compatible

Constant control, analysis and improvement are intended to gradually produce more and more knowledge to be inserted into the ongoing processes. In the course of this knowledge expansion, the area of ignorance is considered to become constantly smaller. Moreover, closely connected to this understanding of knowledge expansion is the idea that in the end all uncertainties will be resolved. Modern hopes of steadily growing knowledge are often expressed in the presupposition that the world is calculable and thus mathematically describable. Mathematicians themselves – think of Kurt Gödel and his Incompleteness Theorem – will rarely share this naive interpretation of their discipline. Furthermore, the mathematical methods in QM are far from being able to nourish such hopes.

And so QM does not describe the (corporate) world with the help of mathematics, but conversely elements of the corporate world are – even though indeed counted and proportioned – freely interspersed in mathematical operations at will. If through this endeavour so-called "zero-defect" processes are calculated, does this not have much to do with error-free processes, as we shall see below.

2. The zero-defect problem I: The Black Belt as nitpicker

The promise to be able to calculate error-free processes in QM is often sold together with the hopes of a Far Eastern spirituality. And so there are some varieties of QM in which course participants receive badges of rank adapted from Japanese martial arts. The participant starts off, for example, as a white belt, then advances via the green belt and the black belt to become finally a Master Black Belt.

Costly initiation rites define the advancement. The reward for all these efforts is not only the promise of being able to create zero-defect processes in the end, but on top of this to belong to an elite caste.[10] Apart from these promises of salvation they also hold out the prospects of fantastic profits, garnished with all sorts of analyses and calculations.

Now it is certainly easy to describe mere technical processes in a mathematically correct and error-free way. However, as soon as staff and client come into play and through this also social, psychological and communicative aspects, it is not possible to carry out clear calculations. In "zero-defect processes" there is an attempt to approach this problem not with Far Eastern wisdom but with pragmatic solutions. In order to achieve this, first of all the demand to capture all work processes in their complexity is given up. Instead, relatively arbitrary parameters that allow for measurable operations are determined. The question of whether these parameters are of importance for the respective working process is not in focus.

The special definition of "quality" in QM opens many doors for this approach; accordingly, quality is already given if only the requirements are met. In the quality measurement of, for instance, nursing processes, you do not reflect the question whether or not a patient receives sufficient attention and a fully health-promoting treatment, because this can hardly be measured. You consider what can be measured –

---

[10] But here they overlook the fact that even W.E. Deming, the possibly most significant father of QM, already described such elitist excesses as counterproductive to successful QM processes. And not only that – Deming, the decisive co-developer of the statistical process control methods, did not deny the problem of seemingly elegant statistical calculations for complex situations, unlike many of his emulators. In Deming (1988: 486), he introduces a chapter by citing Euripedes' *The Bacchae* – "Do not confuse your wits with wisdom", and immediately takes it *ad absurdum* with the following quote from the same work: "Wisdom sounds foolish to fools". The following quote also indicates that Deming was able to assess a genuine system of seemingly constantly increasing knowledge more like a Black Belt. Deming uses this quotation from Ecclesiastes (1:18) to introduce the chapter 12 of his book: "For in much wisdom is great grief: and he that increaseth knowledge increaseth sorrow" (Deming 1988: 371).

like how many (measurable) times the patient received how many (countable) injections and how many body-washing processes were carried out. The corresponding "quality of nursing" is then defined on the basis of such counts, and in the following zero-defect process presumably already screened by a Green Belt.

A striking example illustrates this: A "zero-defect process" could be defined that every patient of a particular group receives an exactly determined and measurable number of nursing units per day. And the definition of "zero-defect nursing quality" can thus be arbitrarily positioned on the lowest level. Let us say that the new definition determines two nursing units instead of formerly common three units. Now if the employees do not make any – or hardly any – more mistakes with regard to the trimmed requirements in our example, then we hardly count any errors, of course.

In order to still impress with this circular argument, in the "zero-defect processes" it is blown up with statistical terms and may then sound like this: Assuming normally distributed process data[11], a "zero-error-process-target" is reached, if the mean of the observed values is within the upper and lower specification limits and if it is at least six (if not seven or eight) standard deviations away from both specification limits. In this situation, even if the mean drifts by 1.5 standard deviations over the course of time, the probability of an error (i.e., the probability of values outside of the specification limits) is at most 0.0000034%.

This sounds far more impressive! Useless arithmetical games of this kind do not only include the problems of measurement I to III (see chapter IV, section 2). They reduce the whole aspired "zero-error mathematics" to a nitpicking endeavour dishonourable to every Black Belt. The most important thing is not even tried from the onset. An exact description of the processes and the possibility to improve the

---

[11] Let us forget here that the process results in QM are not necessarily normally distributed.

quality of the processes in "zero-defect processes" is in fact incidental. The processes are not expected to happen error-free with respect to commonly accepted standards but only to the self-determined criteria, regardless of how differentiated they may be. Quality within QM is in the end no more than the fulfilment of the set standards. It is measuring what was made measurable in advance in a bizarre way. Minimal error probabilities are not yielded from decreasing errors in the processes, but they are solely products of the ludicrous measurement design. The measurement dogma of QM "You can only improve what is measurable" is thus reversed: "If mistakes are not measurable in the way expected by a Master Black Belt, then these errors do not exist …"

3. The zero-defect problem II: Trapped in the past

Continuous improvement could be so nice. Due to the prior analysis, the solution of all problems is produced almost automatically. Non-knowledge would decrease to the extent the knowledge increases and eventually there are only zero-defect processes worthy of the name. In practice, this simplified model fails where it becomes a little bit complex – considering the complex processes in an organization, more or less everywhere. But also in theory, we can explain why the failure of such a truncated way of thinking is ultimately unavoidable.[12]

---

[12] In 1931, the above-mentioned mathematician Kurt Gödel already proved the impossibility of formal axiomatizations for arithmetic. According to this, a non-contradictory system of corresponding mathematical statements is at the same time incomplete, because it contains at least one statement that cannot be proven within the system. The paradox of analysis illustrates the fact that conceptual analysis cannot be correct at the same time as being informative (through changes/improvements):
If the *analysans* (the expression to be analysed) has the same meaning as the *analysandum* (the expression that is supposed to be analysed), then the expression is correct. However, the analysis then only claims what every language user knows in advance. If the analysis is informative, then the

The above cycle of continuous improvement implies the idea that new knowledge or the improvement can easily be fitted into the existing and past-oriented knowledge. The cycle works as long as the new adds to the already existing knowledge. But what happens if new knowledge and given knowledge are not compatible? Image 8 demonstrates such a situation.

The cycle cannot be sustained in a situation where the arduously acquired improvements are not compatible any longer with the formerly given knowledge. Then we get into a clearly paradoxical situation:

- If the new knowledge/improvement is evaluated as correct ("error-free"), then the old knowledge was wrong.

- Yet, originally wrong knowledge cannot give rise to new, correct (and "error-free") knowledge.

- Therefore, innovative knowledge cannot develop in this process itself, but must be introduced from the outside into the process.

- Knowledge without viable anchoring in existing knowledge can only be perceived as an error.

Philosophy of Science. Self-reference is then not only problematic – for its tautology – but also stands for the inherent rightness of an intellectual concept. The knowledge in such a cycle was used in its development and was also transferred to other areas of knowledge. Conversely, the new knowledge occurs at first only as something unpleasant in appearance, as an error. The old knowledge, oriented in the

---

analysans cannot have the same meaning as the *analysandum*. In this case, the analysis is incorrect. (after philex.de, access 27/01/2003).

past, is generally stronger than the new knowledge, which is oriented to an uncertain future.

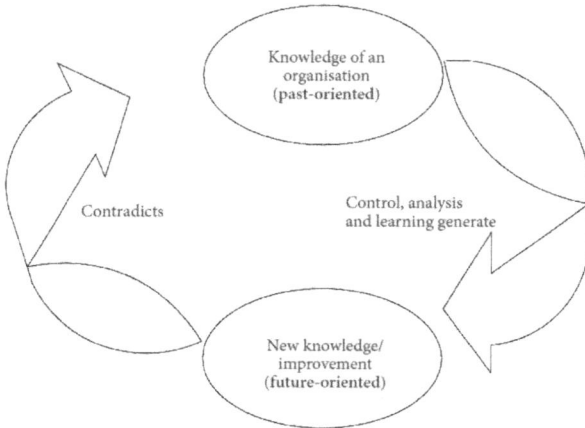

Image 8: The cycle of continuous improvement – improvement and given knowledge are incompatible

When in the early Middle Ages the idea arose that the Earth is not flat like a disk but may be a round object that turns around its own axis, the people were not aware of what would become possible with this new approach. They first saw that logically giving up the idea of the disk would also mean questioning other convictions. For example, the old idea that the universe orbits around the earth and humans was also believed to prove their position in the divine order. This divine order with humankind at the centre of being was the established way of thinking at that time. New knowledge that would question this order could only be wrong.

Today we believe to know that the Earth is not exactly a ball but indeed spherical. This idea has proven to be correct.

Unlike our ancestors, we do not consider the idea of the spherical shape to be a scandalous fallacy and delusion. In retrospect, this idea appears to us like a "stroke of genius", a "flash of wit", a "divine spark" ushering in a paradigm shift in science. This is what happens almost always to the ingenuous new idea. It needs space in order to explain itself. It takes time until an alleged error turns into a ground-breaking, paradigmatic event that turns things upside-down (and eventually again downside-up).

It is all too obvious that the more complex a given knowledge system is, the fewer the opportunities to cause a genuine paradigm shift. The more good arguments support such a system, the less its basic assumptions are questioned – an idea similarly seditious as that of the spherical shape of the earth would hardly become accepted today. This is just like in QM, with its complex processes of differentiation, where they hang on the same logic forever.

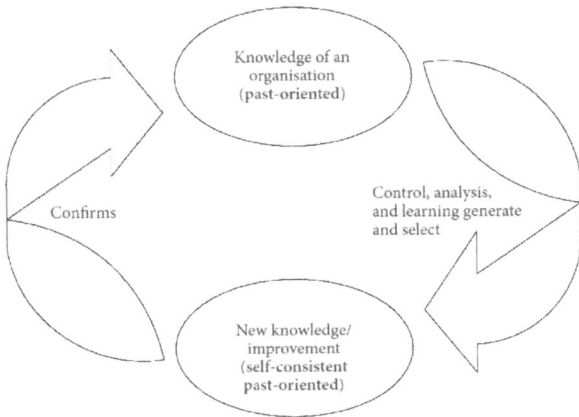

Image 9: The cycle of continuous improvement in highly differentiated processes – improvement and given knowledge – are interdependent

If new knowledge once really bothers an existing, highly differentiated reasoning cycle, it is just a question of short time until everything would again be back to "error-free" normal. The given knowledge can only increase eventually if really new knowledge does not prevent this, but instead is selected early enough.

In modern Organization Theory, the problem that old knowledge impedes the emergence of new knowledge is made responsible for momentous fallacies. Taking into account the "logic of the past", it is factually and technically quite correct that managers manoeuvred themselves into a blind alley, risking the existence of their companies. The banking crisis of 2008 is a dramatic example of this problem. In the crisis, the long-term valid cost-benefit-logic showed its true colours. In the context of circular fallacies, the chairman of IBM, T.J. Watson, is often referenced. The following remark is attributed to him (1943): "I think there is a world market for maybe five computers". Or citing Ken Olsen, the co-founder of the Digital Equipment Corporation (DEC), who still said in 1977: "There is no reason for any individual to have a computer at home" (Gausemeier et al. 1995: 84). Both computer experts were caught in their old knowledge – having stood the test of time, but past-oriented – that other possibilities seemed completely quixotic to them.

In this way, the complete knowledge of an organization can also be trapped in the past through self-reference. Organization Theory of the 1980s discussed in detail the cultivation of self-reference. Organizational theorists did not regard the lack of knowledge any more as the problem that impeded innovation and progress. The "too good memory", the existing knowledge, they argued, was to be blamed for the failure of planning projects of companies and administrations. After all, the knowledge in organizations does not have much in common with the mathematical and scientific knowledge established over centuries. Rather, it is a fragile entity formed by the zeitgeist, individual preferences and arbitrariness. With each step that is simply fitted into existing knowledge patterns, organizations increasingly tie themselves down on existing structures and processes. And then these stand in the way of innovative learning steps. A good memory that stores knowledge of the past in a well-structured way opposes future change. As a consequence, organization theorists advised managers to train oblivion. The existing papers, evaluations and calculations of an organization should thus be recognized and treated as a "plague". Instead of reading from conventionally correct standards, future-oriented planning should better "read from caribou bones" – after the model of Canadian hunters (Weick 1985: 373).

Whether it is really wise to regard all existing knowledge as threatening is another question. What becomes clear, however, is that the clinging to the past can reach alarming levels in the increasingly differentiating knowledge in QM. With each differentiation step, you receive another good confirmation of the old knowledge. Real innovations have no real chance in a differentiated self-reference. Nothing is more threatening for a company than unreeling the determined and, in the worst case, "error-free" processes. No matter how much we summon the necessary changes, dynamic progress and continuous improvement in today's QM systems. Every day, a new amount of self-referential rules is defined. There is simply no escape.

IV. Modern quality management (QM) and its consequences

1. How QM demotivates employees

1.1. The role of employees in QM

Employees are generally assigned to the "resources" in QM systems. This puts them on the same significance level as the infrastructure (buildings, mechanical processing equipment, etc.) and the feedstock. They are to be managed together with the rest of the "material". Furthermore, in QM concepts that give more rhetorical significance to the employees, the inclusion of employees happens in practice always the same way:

- The bases in QM planning for quality-managed processes are the obvious structures and the already existing knowledge written down (descriptions of workplaces and work processes).

- In a first work step the employees are then asked to explicate the descriptions. The work processes are to be described as differentiated as possible. The employees should add, in particular, the knowledge that is not yet present in the descriptions.

- In order to get the knowledge out of the employees and into the processes in a new way, work groups, quality circles, or CIP groups are formed.[13]

- The subsequent step – for instance, the detailed description of work and production processes in the form of a QM handbook – is generally produced by

---

[13] CIP stands for "continual improvement process".

QM personnel. The majority of process steps are thereby determined as "standard", as the norm which is binding from now on. The standards are meant to be measurable with the help of ratios. An administrative work process can, for example, contain the standard of "control of the application data". This standard could be measured with the indicator "time necessary for the control of the application data per application".

- After the planning phase, it is the employees' job and duty to carry on with the process steps as required, thus to keep up with the standards. Furthermore, they have to collect the ratio measurements and further documentation for the data basis, with the help of which later control and further improvements shall take place.

To summarize, the role of the employees in QM – after the introductory sessions that still include them (which may be repeated in times of crises) – is predominantly to keep up and document the standards. In fact, control and the possibilities to decide are to be moved on from the employee to the management level. In this respect, QM representatives often like to promise managers that they would now have the possibility of control in their hands more than ever. Today's wildly popular "management by objectives" seems to become only an "adjustable screw" with the aid of standards and ratios that can be slightly turned up or down at will by the top bosses.

1.2. Unavoidable, general employee problems

Already in the first survey phase in a QM process, the employees are required not only to have strong nerves, but also to invest time resources – and this is usually out of all proportion to the results. The obvious and simplest procedures are documented laboriously in a written form. It is diligently written down again what has already been written for a long time. Sometimes the QM process is already over after this introduction phase. The employees now know exactly what they already knew and can resume their work. If, however, the quality engineers dedicate themselves to the continuous improvement approach, the employees have to sacrifice even more time for documentation. Instead of using machines, completing administrative procedures, curing patients, serving customers, and teaching students, employees are preoccupied with more important matters aiming for continuous improvement – namely, with the precise measurement of the different components of all these processes to be continuously repeated!

According to research by the Marburg Union (Marburger Bund) the emigration of many doctors from Germany is not caused by poor pay and long working hours in the clinics. Instead, it is the documenting of their work that drives this occupational group to flee. Most of them have to deal with management activities many hours every day (cf. ÄrzteZeitung 22/12/2009).

In order to provide that employees are at least able to meet their actual tasks to a certain extent, we now find independent departments for "quality assurance" established in almost all large companies. With the help of old and always new methods (FMEA,[14] audits, BSC,[15] benchmarking, CIA,[16] CMMI,[17] SPC,[18] QFD,[19] data mining...), these departments can control, evaluate, document and count with strength and maintain everything that only seems to be suitable for this venture. It only lies in the nature of things that in the end in the "quality departments", the rest of the staff are less relieved

---

[14] Failure Mode and Effects Analysis

[15] Balanced Scorecard

[16] Cross-Impact Analysis

[17] Capability Maturity Model Integration

[18] Statistical Process Control

[19] Quality Function Deployment

of quality tasks. Instead, this is where an impact force for new measurements and documentation tasks develops undisturbed.

Nonetheless, unfortunately there is not only the inevitable energy guzzler for the employees called "data collection and measurement". Even after the precise, differentiated design of work processes it is unavoidable that questions, doubts, failures or any kinds of possible errors occur. The more complex a work process, the greater the likelihood that at some point disturbances appear. In complex processes, disorders are likely to occur from the beginning. When hospital patients in admission do not want to do the standard tests, when students at a grade level have not yet understood the material that was standard the previous school year, when insurance clients want individual conditions... the whole brave new world of standardization has gone to pieces long before an employee can get into action and meet quality and ratio requirements.

What now is the situation for the employees like if they want to treat such disorders quickly and efficiently? Process descriptions are ultimately no proposals for action but "standards" – precisely what was formerly called "rules". By committing the staff to standards that did not exist before the introduction of QM, their scope of decision-making is clearly limited. However, it is exactly decisions that must be taken in such ambiguous situations.

What can employees do who realize in the middle of a process that – due to poor planning, of changing conditions, etc. – something goes basically wrong? To solve the problem with an individual decision, will often mean in QM that the process rules, the standards are violated. Correctly, the employee would therefore have to appeal to the next higher level in the hierarchy and ask there for a decision.

Middle management, however, tends to be abolished in QM processes. In the end, we have instead the many ratios that do not only serve the orientation of employees. Invisible ratio threads are designed to ensure that work processes are performed exactly as they were planned in detail in the complex survey phase. The QM rhetoric of "self-determination", "participation", "individualization" or even "empowerment" ultimately means that employees check their work performance very personally and privately in the strictest manner. Problems are not planned in this context.

Therefore, they are usually ignored bravely in "mature" processes.[20] Problems of all kinds would in fact otherwise have to be transported from the bottom up (such as the knowledge of the employees before the process definitions) – only so that they can then finally be decided upon by the top line and be sent down again. This is, in general, even too silly for the supervisor. And the employees will – in order to stay a little capable of acting – bypass the entire processing of QM, the whole work in order to rule and make their own decisions. Sure, then they have to risk order warnings, complaints, etc. – even up to legal penalties.

The energy of the employee is thus consumed in QM to a large extent in senseless quality circle sessions, in the measuring procedures of any kind, unsolved problems and unclear decision-making situations. What still remains then cannot only be inserted in feelings of guilt and fear due to the necessary "standard" transgressions. Because besides these general problems triggered by QM, they have to master, in particular, the following.

1.3. Concentration on the thumbscrews: the central employee problem in QM

We know this phenomenon already from Science Theory. It has been described a hundred times with always the same example: with the "butterfly's fluttering" which in the course of a causal chain causes a storm. Small causes can have great effects. In QM now the simple turning of one screw, of the

---

[20] In chapter III, section 3, it was shown how the ignorance of problems is made possible in differentiated QM processes.

target values of the standards and ratios, should end in a true storm of increased employees' efforts, in more products that are even better than the old ones, in higher profits and finally fulminant listings on the stock exchanges.

"One goal of improvement that the management could, for example, demand is to double the margin within a defined time frame with the help of the model. The increasing of the margin leads to increasing employees' motivation..." (Simon & Janzen 2001: 1172). This is how easy management in QM works. And so be it that the employees moan and groan instead of showing motivation. The QM responsible will soothe the unsettled manager: "This is where we have to bring them. They have to withstand this..." But which storm now is caused by such a small turn of the screw? Who in the end pays the higher price for manipulating the screws and for the guidance with ambitious goals shall be analysed in more detail in the following.

The "QM resource employees" are human beings and therefore their physical and psychological capacities are limited. This fact creates natural limits to the constantly increasing efforts. Employees, however, also bring other qualities: knowledge, flexibility, creativity, and intelligence to be applied. In QM it is not only believed that the knowledge of employees could be captured and inserted without any problem into the process descriptions. But it is also assumed that this knowledge can be stored there and anchored like a real treasure.

Everybody who knows a bit about knowledge can already suspect the dimensions of the inevitable collapse that such a cocktail of myths and fantasies of omnipotence causes. The access to their knowledge in a work area that employees have is incomparably more direct that that of any QM auditor. When the screws get turned, the employees will know how to protect themselves. Certainly, the employees will meet the planned target, but not overdo it. In order not to get harmed, they can tread different paths. Smart employees will already have shown the appropriate commitment in the process of the planning of the dreaded norms and standards: "You have to fight them with their own weapons and think about every step, every movement you do carefully before. Always do a little more and a little more slowly, follow all the security instructions... Only if you take all your brain substance you can avoid that they wear you out", says a worker (own interview collection) in an industrial company about the measurements of the QM engineers.

Even if after the first planning phase all requirements have been described in detail, there are enough ways for employee manipulation to take place. The "tunnel vision", for example, allows handling senseless requirements without a problem. Then employees will only do what the standard proposes and what increases the performance indicators. We can observe something bizarre at universities in this respect. If there is money given – for example, as part of a "performance-based" allocation of research funds mostly to those who can show most publications in specified journals in a certain period of time – then we can imagine what researchers spend their time on.

It may also be due to the tunnel vision of teachers that students in schools learn less now than before times of the Pisa study. They mainly teach what will also be tested. When citizens complain about incompetent consulting and decision-making in public administrations, then we should not forget that the employees have to leave aside all those aspects of their competence that are not measured afterwards. Why should an employee take care of a complicated planning application, if it matters more for them to work through the highest number possible of applications in a week?

The tunnel vision of the dreaded "service according to the rules" used previously by employers is only one possibility for reaching naively constructed goals. Also small manipulations of the statistics are not the exclusive right of the QM personnel. Anyone can participate in data tampering, fantasy measurements and imaginary counting. And who will prove that counselling employees have in fact not worked with 69 of their data protected clientele but only 34 instead? And who will seriously send a reminder to a worker in the final inspection that out of the 1,000 necessary focus controls they only carried out 600? The simple "checking the boxes" is an extremely popular strategy in QM that still allows mastering extensive forms at the end on all process levels.

As a third method to meet the so-called "management by objectives" it is suitable to simply imaginatively reinterpret the specifications and the standards. Again, the QM engineers show how this works (see, e.g., chapter IV, section 3.9). Consider, for example, the standard "detailed discussion with the new customers", which lasted on average 20 minutes before the QM measures and was then not fixed in length. Employees now who suffer the screw twists very much will interpret the term "detailed" individually and so drive away potential customers after just five minutes. Even if a teacher has to raise the "individual support" standard that is then controlled by the indicator of "number of pupils who do not pass the year", he can document the achievement of this standard entirely at his own discretion. In the end, the teacher can just let more pupils pass and can thus demonstrate the achievement of objectives.

The creativity, knowledge and intelligence of employees are squandered in QM in the "services according to the rules" (even tunnel vision has to be first learned by motivated employees) via the requisite small and large statistical fraud and reinterpretations and redefinitions of the macabre new world of standards. Sometimes employees can even save a little genuine quality for themselves, for the organization and for the customers. Mostly, however, it is clear who foots the medium and long-term bill for the steady, further rotation of the adjustable screws. But companies do not only dig their own graves in this way. QM still holds next to the obligatory problem programme for employees some other options. These are considered in the following paragraphs.

1.4. Ridiculing and blackmailing of employees in QM

In QM it is often assumed that the employee – if only everything is wrapped in nice words – does not even really notice what is going on. So says a QM guru: "If management wants to increase business productivity, the union will ask: 'Why is this so? That will basically only mean that we need to work harder. What do we get from it?' No one, however, can be against quality, not even the unions" (Masaaki Imai 1998: 130).

Here a further attempt will be made to sell the differentiated process descriptions to nurses as an opportunity for "professionalization" ("like this you can see at least what you are doing..."). Workers are made believe that it is now finally time to end the separation of manual and intellectual work at their expense. It is explained to employees that the many new rules would make everything much more transparent and that this transparency would indeed ultimately serve their own safety ("Then you can always say that you have done everything right..."). And they are all together told something about simplification (under the differentiated surface) and about the future, which consists of consummate quality, of zero-error processes and excellence. The real socialist 5-year planners whose boldest quality rhetoric did not go far beyond the "heroes of labour" and the "over-fulfilment of the planned targets" would, in view of such statements, have become green with envy.

Yes, even the fusion of labour and capital in QM rhetoric is no longer a problem! With the help of the concept of "internal customers" any contradiction can here be avoided: The internal customers of a company are in fact not those who end up buying a product in the company's premises, no, the internal customers are the colleagues. An employee should treat his or her colleagues as courteous as customers should be treated. But above all, quality expectations and quality requirements of the internal customer-colleagues should be fully satisfied ("like in actual real life" you are tempted to add here). The product is both the result of the employees' labour and a product they sell. In the concept of "internal customers" every employee is a customer/buyer of the products and also a business owner/seller of those products at the same time. The request of the customer's internal colleagues for "goods perfectly appropriate to the standards" then means the complete fusion of corporate interests and employee interests....

The stultification of employees with such concepts is often only the start of the increase of this strategy. Thus, standards are, for example, artificially increased by conscious errors and false measurements. In a university hospital, employees were forced to improve their performance statistics in this manner. They were kindly requested to orient their performance statistics to departments where more favourable values were measured. Embellished performance records put employees under pressure and let a company seem better to the outside world than it actually is. But if the default values move to unrealistic heights, the employee will have to override these values to meet the real needs of the operational process. The supervisors will largely tolerate these rule violations, which is also in their interest. The unrealistic standards then provide an effective means for any disciplining and extortion. In cases of conflict, the supervisors may rely on the given rules and standards and insist on their compliance and sanction non-compliance.

And what happens if, despite all attempts at brainwashing and blackmailing, the targeted standards and ratio values are not even achieved with tricks and by turning a blind eye? What if the employee problems turn out to be more and more obviously business problems? Yes, it is the scolding from the ranks of quality engineers that workers and employees and in particular the remaining cursed middle management should only "get really involved". Then the golden age could dawn in which the quality management works as promised in the glossy brochures (cf. Kalbfleisch et al. 2001).

1.5. The sorcerer's apprentices: How employee problems in QM produce more and more business problems

Employees do not only take the largest proportion of their time but also their commitment and motivation every morning to the company. And since there are hardly any people who want to waste their valuable resources, companies, administrations, hospitals and universities could have a viable and resilient foundation from them that is reliable even in difficult times.

But what happens if the employees are treated as described above? What if they are spoon-fed and unnecessarily controlled? If they are not even taken seriously by the naive QM rhetoric and if they even get imposed the scapegoat function for the undeniable misconduct of the QM? We have already seen the way in which QM-stricken employees can use their energies in other ways. The requirements are met to a high price for the organization, for quality and customer.

But thus, the blocking capabilities of employees are not exploited yet to their full extent. The everyday work life provides the employees at all levels of the hierarchy with a wealth of opportunities to invest their valuable time in revenge of any kind (cf. Reinker 2007). If QM spoon-fed employees only "work to rule" with the help of tunnel vision, their dedication and initiative stay behind. Even if the standards are easily achieved, employees who have "terminated internally", do not want to waste their spare capacities. They will withdraw from thinking about corporate issues that do not belong in their closer responsibility descriptions. Through failure to complete, by doing nothing, dawdling and silent refusals the employees have the possibility in their hand to repay their employer paternalism by QM and QM harassment in the simplest way. Office staffs, for example, only need a little practice in the discipline of "pretence of work" and then wily QM representatives do not even unmask them. In the relevant literature (cf. Maier 2006, Adams 2003), employees find enough evidence as to how they can appear busy without actually doing anything, through:

- continuous complaints about work stress,

- the constant carrying of heavy documents (also in the hallway to the cafeteria and when chatting with colleagues),

- the harried, late show-up at sessions ("I have just come from XY..."),

- leaving early the same session, stricken with grief facial expression,

- the taking of files in the evening and especially on weekends,

- sending out mass e-mails, etc.

Those who believe that these frustrated employees are exceptional cases will be disappointed. According to a survey of the German Trade Union (DGB)[21] on the testimony of more than 6,000 employees in 2007, over a third assessed their working situation as "poor". In 2015 the consulting company Gallup even arrives at more than two thirds of all employees who have internally so far distanced themselves from their company that they only make the call of duty. Around 16% have terminated internally according to this study.

Given these figures, it is no surprise that employees still find even different ways for their silent refusal in the form of idleness, excessive absenteeism and handling private matters at work (browsing the Internet, calling friends, working on private matters...). Often employees are also willing to actively work against the interests of their company. For activities to the detriment of employers there are many possibilities available. They can "forget" to pass on important information.

---

[21] DGB stands for *German Deutscher Gewerkschaftsbund.*

There can be rumours initiated and serious computational errors are "accidentally" incorporated into crucial documents. And there the employees turn the major screws a little in the corporate process to secretly cause sabotage and blockages. In the computer age, it is already possible using a few clicks to erase hard drives and to distribute viruses.... Experts suggest that frustrated employees triggered many a misfortune – from a plane crash to the nuclear accident. In that the timing of revenge is right – meaning the humiliation and revenge can hardly be pinned on outsiders – the responsible party is usually not discernible.

Finally, employees may receive small compensation for humiliation suffered by the theft of material, ideas and knowledge. Moreover, this strategy of employees that ensures that QM impositions are vehemently rejected is not only applied in exceptional cases. Theft of knowledge is usually more problematic for companies: the higher the theft employee in the hierarchy, the more he or she also has exclusive access to crucial information.

And if nothing helps in the end, people do not flinch to open and actively take action against their employer. In addition to the invocation of labour courts, going public is an effective means to offer the (former) employer a good counterpoint. "Whistle-blowers" are informants who make illegal activities public that happen within their organization. Especially in the context of an ever more pervasive delusion of regulatory and quality requirements, not only workers but also organizations can make more and more mistakes. The public is then grateful to be informed thoroughly about the many cases of non-compliance with the alleged quality in companies and administrations.

2. How QM leads to the loss of knowledge in a company

People in QM like to feel surrounded by an aura of precision and impeccability. A special proximity to science, technology and mathematics is thereby suggested. The general acceptance and approval that findings in science have shall thus also be available in QM.

However, there is a major difference if we only strive for the temporarily realizable reduction of expenses, the increase of profits or if we are interested in actual, lasting knowledge. In QM the impartial look at the situation is averted by an ideologically blurred filter right from the beginning. Not those facts that have also been proven by independent science get acknowledged and accepted in QM, but an arbitrary status quo is taken as the unquestionable point of departure of all assessments. Accordingly, "knowledge" in QM is a very special material that does not have much in common with the generally approved knowledge.

Nonetheless, the loss of knowledge in QM follows similar rules as the unavoidable loss of knowledge in science. However, if we describe these rules in the following, we should be aware of a crucial difference between QM and science. In science it has been common from the beginning to describe and reflect the problems in knowledge theory. The loss of knowledge has not only been criticized in various ways, but it has also been brought to light and illuminated. The processes of knowledge loss transferred to QM in the following subsections relates to those descriptions. But before this we shall take a look at the problem of measurement.

2.1. The measurement problem I: Measurement means relativization

In QM, it is not the evaluation but the measurement that gets a central significance: "What cannot be measured cannot be improved", is often stated in QM publications. This heavy statement lets us sense the roots of QM, which are grounded in engineering sciences. What is not measurable can actually not exist.

The measurement, though, is not necessarily proof of the existence of something. Because in every measurement there is a problem: You can always only measure in relation to something else. Length is, for example, measured in relation to the original prototype meter stored in Pairs. A litre is also only meaningful with relation to a specified amount of liquid that has been determined arbitrarily.

At first sight, the measured amount of nutrients in today's quality foods seems to mean something. But the quality of a quality sausage with a certain number of nutrients can only be evaluated if we know the amount of nutrients in other foods, if we know the daily need of nutrients; if we know about the availability of biological nutrients in a quality sausage; if we have information about the biochemical backgrounds (in the sausage, in other food, in our body), etc.

It is obvious that quality is often relative. But is this also true for the dominant units to which the measurement of quality is today often reduced, such as, for example, velocity, money and time? These seemingly absolute values are only meaningful in relation to something else, a second value. With velocity this second thing is the combination of distance and time. Similarly, money in itself is only printed-on paper. And an hour is only measurable because we put it in relation to something else, namely the movement of the planets.

Well, even in the media of measurement itself, in the numbers, this problem exists. Numbers by themselves do not mean anything. Only in relation to (countable) things or at least to other numbers do they make sense. This problem drove generations of philosophers and mathematicians to despair. How shall existence be explained without relation to non-existence? How shall the number one be explained without relation to zero?

The conclusion is always the same: We can only measure in relation to a second element, which again can only be determined in relation to the invisible third element etc. In other words: Measurement is a comparison based on other comparisons. Measurement is constant relativization. Hard facts are softened under this perspective.

2.2. The measurement problem II: Not everything that is countable counts and not everything that counts is countable (Albert Einstein)

Even in QM there is an attempt to find out if the thing that is actually measured is the same thing that should be measured. A survey on the satisfaction of customers, for example, only tells us something if in fact the satisfaction of the customers is measured. The combination of such a survey with price competitions, coupon distribution and free tickets will also have a result, but not necessarily the assessment of customer satisfaction.

In order to find out the right measurement values, the following questions should be answered:

- What is the indispensable core of a product or a work process?
- Which features determine it?
- What is the weight of these features in relation to each other and to other process components?
- How can we construct indicators with which these single features can be measured?

For processes with a simple structure, thus those for which we can determine the central components without any doubt, it seems to be simple to determine the right thing. But generally speaking, nobody is interested in the obvious or trivial facts. In complex processes the answers to the questions above open eternal possibilities for errors. Resuming all four questions, we have to determine the most important factor. In complex processes we have the obstacle that different observers also judge differently with respect to the most important factor in a process. Also in the course of time, the priorities shift, and what formerly seemed important is void and small at once. If for example, a type of food is sold well or not, does not only depend on the way how it is produced, but on the flavour, the ingredients and how many calories it has. Now aspects increasingly play a role that people did not care about in the past: Is it organic or not? Can it be related to a fashion in the area of health and lifestyle? The same holds for the analysis of work processes. The most important factor is often only notable at a second or third glance. It is disputable, changing through time and with the observer.

We often attempt to find the most important factor in a process where the obvious problems lie. However, we can also get lost with a view that is problem-oriented, since the view on the other part that works without problem is obstructed and the most important factor fades into the background. If, for example, the management of the German Railways moans about the low number of high-velocity direct trains, relating them directly with expectable profits, and if they thus move the side rail tracks out of the attention, then they ignore the close relativity of one to the other. Without enough functioning side rail tracks there can also not be enough users of the high-velocity trains.

Even when we believe that we have found the important factor, then this does not mean that this makes it visible. The question through which features it can be determined is often hard to answer. A carpenter who is a good craftsman will fix all his work processes in a differentiated way. And still, it will often not be possible for another carpenter to reach the same results with his descriptions. In Organization Theory, we therefore distinguish "explicit knowledge" (knowledge that can be made visible) and "implicit knowledge" (knowledge that cannot be made visible or only partially). The more complex work processes are, the more implicit knowledge is generally included.

In the modern division of labour we do not only distinguish between mental and physical work, but also rank mental work higher than physical labour. And the mental workers are, of course, involved in a hierarchy. On the one hand, control shall come from top to bottom. On the other, in order to make this work, the knowledge has to be transmitted from bottom to top: implicit knowledge has to be made explicit. In QM, the demands on the extension and velocity of this knowledge transfer has increased. Everything that is significant shall not only be differentiated, but also fixed in its flexibility and dynamics.

In complex processes, these demands quickly reach the limits. Such a controllability will also in future remain an illusion. Sometimes reaching the implicit knowledge is tried through different forms of employee's participation (quality circles, CIP teams). Quality strategies, however, are closely connected to the increasing goals and control and are carried out with planned work dismissals. And it is thus not surprising if progress in the process of the conversion of implicit to explicit knowledge is also actively prevented by the involved knowledge parties.

The most important factor is therefore not only difficult to detect, disputable and changeable, but it is often not possible to make it visible and it will frequently intentionally be kept unmentioned. For various reasons, measurement processes happen therefore mostly in places where the most important factor is not present any more, in places where numbers can be collected, without being too demanding on the measuring instruments. It happens in places that offer material for communication, for which all participants are already prepared. In like manner, we prefer looking for our glasses in the light of the cosy living room lamp instead of in the dark cellar, where we were wearing them last.

2.3. The measurement problem III: The fallacy of quality measurements

The old engineer's wisdom "who measures mis-measures" does not only refer to the measurement problem II, but also to the fallacy of quality measurements. In the following we describe three measurement mistakes that are particularly frequent: the simply wrong measurement, the wrong measurement influenced by the measurement situation, and the deficient representation of the measured data. The first one, the classical possibility of wrong measurement, is caused by deficient measurement instruments and by intentional or unintentional errors of the person measuring. These errors occur easily, but they are often difficult to correct. Everybody will know the story about spinach supposedly being rich of iron. Generations of children were forced to eat this vegetable – and the story was retold even long after it was found that the iron contained in spinach was measured incorrectly. The salvation of such wrong measurements unfortunately does not come about by finally measuring correctly. If presumed "knowledge" has once been let free into the world, then it is difficult to erase it again, even with the best proofs, as we have seen in chapter III, section 3.

The next cause for wrong measurements has not only been addressed in physics, but it has also been discussed in Organization Theory long before the introduction of QM methods. It includes the problem that it is hardly possible to measure complex process features exactly without also changing them during or through this measurement. Particularly during the measurement of human behaviour the measurement situation has an effect on the results. Bodily features, such as temperature and blood pressure, often show different results at the doctor's than at home. Psychological patients will not only show different results in behaviour tests in the psychiatric clinic than at home, but up to that, their answers are influenced by the respective test design to a high degree. And students can fail in a concrete situation in spite of existing knowledge, if the examiner (who is at the same time the "measuring instrument") does not manage to evoke this knowledge.

Also the conscious manipulation of the measured results is not rare in the measuring situation. An administration can, for example, try to measure the commitment of their employees according to the number of cases worked on per week. The number of the completed cases in such a situation will not depend only on the commitment of the employees, but also decisively on the measurement situation. If the employees are afraid to lose their jobs and therefore quite oriented to competition, then the number of completed cases within a week will rise. If in the reverse case, the employees know that they are not simply exchangeable, or if they feel jointly responsible in solidarity for some other reasons, for example in order to avoid later exaggerated requirements, then the completed cases will rather decrease. It is not difficult to comprehend that people who know that they are being observed show different behavioural patterns. Employees will always try to influence the measured results in QM processes.

Of course, also the auditors use the possibility to manipulate the measured results in the measurement situation. Performance tests can be carried out on days where a low workload is expected or when the less efficient employees are absent. The tests can be combined with open or hidden warnings or rewards. Also the tests on the customers satisfaction are generally designed in such a manner that the best values possible can be reached. Not only by means of bonus payments and promotion gifts, but also through the specific wording of the questions and the selection of a good point in time, you can always reach an increase of the satisfaction.

Finally, the third but not less relevant way of inserting errors to a measurement process refers to the analysis of the gained data. Even if everything countable and measurable in a process has been collected and listed by appropriate instruments and reliable personnel, these data cannot directly be reused as planning data. They are analysed and processed, for example with the help of calculating mean values, standard deviations and variances, and they are represented in graphs, bar charts and pie charts.

And again, there are many kinds of possibilities open for bad or wrong representations and, of course, for deliberate manipulation (cf. Krämer 2000). "Data cleansing", for example, enables the deletion of values that deviate to an unwanted degree from the average. Data interpretations open a wide field for influencing the representation of results. Accordingly, you can, for example, express failures "quite correctly" as success. If an interpretation sounds, for instance, like this: "The rate of increase of our new indebtedness has fallen by 3%." Who will then still think that the financial obligation has again increased?

A particularly erroneous data interpretation that continuously makes students of statistics laugh refers to the interconnection of the data results. It will be shown, for example, that the increase of A is related to an increase of B or a decrease of C. The statement: "The decreasing birth rate goes back to the decreasing number of storks" illustrates the problem of mutual relationships or "correlations" that can be derived from statistics.

2.4. Loss of knowledge through the one-dimensional treatment of complexity

QM tries to invoke the impression that it involves the classical analytic thinking that is also applied in the current western science model. This model is based on a treatment of complexity that particularly includes the following convictions:

- *Every effect has its absolutely determinable cause.*

- *Knowledge can be captured in less than 30 letters – in computer language it can be reduced to two numbers: 1 and 0.*

- *The differentiation of a whole into its parts gives us clear insights into the cause-effect relationships.*

Bonding to these convictions is certainly a way to deal with complexity that has its advantages. But it also entails notable disadvantages, uncertainties and contradictions:

- *If every cause has its fixed effects and every effect its determined causes, then people could not act freely, but were determined through all preceding causes. A decision for this or another way would then never be taken, but would have already been done millions of years before. QM would not have any meaning from this perspective. Liberty – and also the liberty of decision, action and planning – has to stay an illusion in this deterministic model. The question of cause and effect belongs to the basic questions in philosophy and cannot be decided here.[22] It is, however, certain that "definitely definable" causes of effects can only be figured out partly in science. Above all, physics is a science in which many cause-effect relationships have proven themselves for centuries.[23]*

- *Also, the correctness of the belief that all knowledge can be captured with the help of language seems plausible at first sight. Language is the instrument we trust most today. However, there are still worlds*

---

[22] The traditional solution to the question, after which only humans are admitted to have a free will and the rest of nature obeys determination, is hardly supported any more today. On the one hand, modern brain science can prove well that also human behaviour is very predictable. On the other, research on primates shows that their free will cannot really be distinguished from that of the human being. Various kinds of freedom of occurrences – often described as "causeless", "initial impulse", "emergence" or "synergy" – can certainly also be supposed outside of organisms (e.g., on the level of the smallest elements). For instance, a very entertaining introduction to this topic was presented by Hondrich (1995).

[23] And even here the question of determination is not at all decided upon. While at the beginning of the last century the theory of quantum mechanics caused some unrest with respect to this topic, today we are asking the question if the so-called constants of nature are immutable. If for example, the smallest parts of material did not at all times have the same mass, so if the physical formulae built upon this cannot be applied, then our currently valid "laws of nature" are in real trouble.

apart between the spoken and intended meaning, between theory and praxis, between fiction and truth.[24] *Also the two signs in computer language, 1 and 0, describe a paradox dilemma.*[25] *Language thus seems to have a sort of ambiguous breaking point, which makes the knowledge captured in it useless in the course of time. Many philosophers were therefore of the opinion that crucial knowledge is only available in a particular form of experience that overcomes this breaking point on a non-verbal level.*[26]

---

[24] Western philosophers tended and still tend to resolve the paradoxical dualism that theory and praxis, language and reality describe, in favour of the side "theory and language". This did not only put the basic paradox in new text forms, but for each contemporary this paradox was made largely invisible. Making paradox constructions invisible even counts as a sign of good theory for many a western philosopher. In contrast, in Buddhism they say: "Buddha hesitated to teach the Dharma, knowing how difficult its profoundness is imagined." Language is radically deconstructed, such as in the form of *koans*. It is important to let the paradox be exposed to the light and let the apprentices also experience the paradoxical emptiness practically and physically:
"Shi-kung: 'Can you grasp emptiness?'
Hsi-t'ang: 'Yes.'
Shih-kung: 'How do you do that?'
Hsi-t'ang closed up his hands around the empty space between them.
Shih-kung: 'But you don't know how you can grasp emptiness.'
Hsi-t'ang: 'How do you do it then?'
Shih-kung grabbed Hsi-t'ang at his nose and pulled it.
Hsi-t'ang: 'Ouch! You are pulling me off my nose!'
Shih-kung: 'This is the only possibility to grasp emptiness.'"
(both citations after Batchelor 2002: 36, 55).
[25] Already Leibnitz, the father of the binary number system, struggled with this paradox and tried to resolve it with his "monadology" under the guiding paradigm of absolute "unity".
[26] Also for Hofstadter it is not the dualistic thinking in words that opposes such an experience, but it is the preceding problem of perception: "As soon as you perceive an object, you draw a line between it and the rest of the world; you divide the world, artificially, into parts you thereby miss the Way" (Hofstadter 1999: 251).

- *The division of the whole into its parts can open up new perspectives. With a little bit of luck you can find cause-effect mechanisms. In chapter II, section 4.3, we have also seen the problems of such a procedure: the number of error possibilities rises with every step of differentiation. Errors result from the wrong description or evaluation of elements, or when mutual dependencies are overlooked, or not even rarely when conscious manipulations are thrown in. Cause-effect mechanisms in a differentiation process are only cause-effect mechanisms until they are replaced by newly discovered cause-effect mechanisms.*

In scientific theory, however, not only the problems of the classical analytical model are described. Likewise, new solutions of epistemological issues emerged. With the help of interpretative theories not only the limits of language were to be elucidated, but also to be made better manageable. "Freedom" and "causelessness" were designed in system theories in a new way, as "emergence" and "openness". Moreover, in chaos theory and concepts of non-linearity and synergy, the question of cause and effect and of the relationship between part and whole appeared in new perspectives.[27]

In QM, though, scientific-theoretical questions are almost ignored completely. Also the classical analytical procedure is hardly taken seriously. Linguistic uncertainties are in QM less

---

[27] In this respect, we should mention in particular the system theory of Niklas Luhmann, which also had influence extending from the narrower limits of philosophy to other disciplines (e.g., to the management theory). In a strong belief in the plausibility of differentiation, Luhmann developed his system theory, which is also often called a "difference theory". In the course of his work, Luhmann met the limits of his belief and therefore performed a paradigm shift (an "autopoietic" turn), where he then focussed on the unity, or the "paradoxical undistinguishable" character of central concepts (cf. Luhmann 1984).

a problem that should be solved, but rather a possibility to blur and reinterpret the meaning content of key concepts. The terms "quality", "value", "customer orientation", and "sustainability" have been deliberately manipulated intentionally and brought to absurdity.

The cause-effect topic gets a similar treatment in QM. Cause-effect relationships are only described in a clear context dependent framework in the organization-theoretical literature. In QM, this condition of the context dependency is, however, less a motivation for more precise observation and examination, but rather it is used as a possibility to justify arbitrary decisions also in arbitrary ways. Nonetheless, cause-effect relationships tend to be described in the form of key performance rationality in QM. If certain "cause values" have been reached, then also the predetermined "effect values" should be achieved. An arbitrary arbitrariness is thus connected to calculations in a specific way (cf. chapter III, section 2).

Calculations on such a basis certainly have their consequences. If students get better results in the Pisa comparative tests than two years before, then we cannot expect that they have become smarter at the same time. Goods and products can truly get worse in their quality and still achieve better ratings. Also in times of financial crisis we have to learn that the first place ratings do not say much about the actual health of banks and companies.

Whenever a whole is disaggregated into its parts, knowledge is getting lost (cf. chapter II, section 4). In science this problem is reduced by probing new knowledge in praxis and supporting it by existing knowledge. This does not seem to be required in QM. Here it is less important to probe carefully each of the dissection patterns than the continuous production of dissections.

The one-dimensional treatment of complexity in QM is therefore at high costs: The possibilities to destroy approved knowledge are not only endless. In QM, we can expect that errors and loss of knowledge are actually realized. Errors would be a much smaller problem if people at least succeeded in fixing the most relevant factors in the differentiated processes. The measurement problem II illustrates that especially in complex social processes, the most relevant factor escapes. It is often not explicitly accessible but part of the implicit knowledge, the instinct, the feeling for the right thing. The more we try to drag it to light, the more data we hold in our hands, the more it is irreparably damaged in the process. In the end we have the complex QM process descriptions with their wholes dissected into such small parts that do not have much to do any more with the whole – parts that have too little validity and too little reliability (cf. measurement problem III). The small parts, into which the processes have been disaggregated, contain particularly small parts. Small parts that start their own lives in the story of the magician's apprentice, lives that cannot be simply ignored in QM, but which are to be put in the place of the "old knowledge".

The unimportant thus becomes more and more important. The wrong gets a place of honour. What counts is banished into the background. The discovery of the most important factor is opposed by the complexity artificially created around it. Nowadays, companies often administer an intranet that may consist of a couple of thousand – or even a hundred thousand – pages. Hence, it especially becomes almost impossible for an employee to find relevant information there.

When it is difficult to detect the really important issue, the call for "knowledge management" is not far away. This, however, does not disrupt the spin-off process of an ever-growing complexity of assumed knowledge. In the framework of knowledge management processes the artificial complexity is increased once again. Today's knowledge managers are certainly not philosophical academics, but they are people who believe strongly in the afore-mentioned convictions. But we cannot extinguish a fire with petrol.

2.5. Loss of knowledge through clinging to false estimations

The downside of the one-dimensional treatment of complexity in QM is not only the loss of the most relevant. The artificial complexity created in the processes contains falsehoods and misunderstanding, thus miscalculations of any kind. How can we explain that these miscalculations resist and exist even after having been proven to be wrong? This question can best be answered with the view on the parallels of QM with the scientific model of thinking. Thus states the critical rationalism: Even though there is no true truth, there are many true untruths – true falsifications.[28]

Now we could point at the fact that these convictions have been questioned in various ways since the beginning of philosophy. Socrates' quote "I know that I don't know anything" proves this just as much as Nietzsche's reference to the paradox of the topic: "There is at least one truth, namely that there is no truth." Also the founder of the critical rationalism, Karl Popper (the father of the above mentioned falsification), argued that science does not have a direct access to "true knowledge". However, he still wanted to continue his examinations without the feeling that it was all for nothing. His theory of science is today in particular applied by experience scientists (empiricists). It does not promise to determine safely the truth but at least the untruth. Popper hid this contradiction that is connected to this promise so well – and made it thus invisible – that many scientists believe this contradiction does not exist at all. If the medical, psychological, and biological science publish their latest findings, if they are praised, and receive Nobel prizes, then hardly anybody notices this worm that lives in all these new

---

[28] The assumption that all swans are white is maintained as long as the appearance of one single black swan falsifies it. On the problem of constructing the "provisional probation" and "falsifications", cf. Warzecha (2004: 61ff.).

results of research (which gets bigger and bigger over the years).[29] Also in QM, the belief in the correctness and truth of the statements of process descriptions is an important reason to stick to them in the future.

This small digression into critical rationalism not only explains the inertia of once gained knowledge. With the help of such models, the empirically founded scientists were able to enter into the mass production of insights. Thus Popper was of the opinion that the true falsities, the "true non-truths" should prove themselves in reality. He could not foresee that also this reality could actually become unreal quite quickly: With the help of manipulated experimental objects and guided frame requirements, the "scientific reality" can also be created arbitrarily nowadays. And should the outcomes not coincide with the expectations, then generous tricks are even common. According to a poll of the US magazine *Nature* in 2005, about a third of all scientists admitted that they sugar-coat their scientific work if needed (cf. Martinson et al. 2005: 737ff.).[30] In this manner more and more knowledge is flooding not only scientific media but also companies and hospitals, administrations and universities. QM procedures are then to fix this "knowledge" and store it.

It is easily understood that wrong estimations which have once been acknowledged the title of "scientific finding" or in QM of "generally accepted standard" cannot simply be corrected. It is also understandable that the false estimations in the sea of new insights cannot be noticed any more. Consider that some scientist believe that the knowledge of humankind has multiplied in the recent years.

And still, we are missing one component for understanding the problem of how knowledge and standards can even then

---

[29] Nassim Nicholas Taleb (2007) describes with many examples the often exponentially growing of such worms, which do not only create problems for the "white swans" of the critical rationalists.

[30] You find a small selection of examples that have become public in the online dictionary *Wikipedia* under the entry "Scientific misconduct".

be deemed as accurate if the opposite has long been known. This missing component has been described in chapter III, section 3. The cycle of knowledge illustrates how once approved knowledge – be it useful or a clear falsity – retains itself. The permanent survival of falsities is assured through the continuous repetition, through alleged probation in praxis and through the paradoxical exclusion of alternatives.

The belief that the Earth is flat has been repeated for centuries. It was seemingly probed – if people watched out, no ship fell off that disk. It was successfully defended against paradoxical alternatives – were the Earth a round planet in the universe, it was not certain any longer that all other planets revolved around it. And this cannot be, since the human being is the centre of creation. Also in QM, false conclusions are kept up through repetition, seeming probation and the exclusion of alternatives, which saves them as standard or norm in an artful way.

In clinics and health insurances that are QM managed we can observe, for instance, the sticking to problematic treatment methods. Medicine, pharmacology and even easier psychiatric medicine and psychology can nowadays "prove" almost anything with the help of numerous experimental guinea pigs and people (it was proved on 4,000 probands ...). Many of these theses stay alive through spreading in the media – hence, through constant repetition. Over the years they become the basis for patient and customer services. And in QM, the more these standards dig deeply into the clinical processes, the more they are newly elaborated in differentiated processes and prescribed and checked (evaluated). Even if the opposite has long been well proven, it is stuck to these false conclusions. In the end, many ill have been cured in spite of these treatments (probation). Today people with a cold, inner ear infection or amygdalitis are still being medicated with antibiotics – even though the usefulness of this treatment has been doubted seriously in the past years and at the same time the damage documented even more. We can say the same about treatment with hormones, painkillers, psychotropic drugs, genes, corticosteroids and chelates. Also various surgical procedures in the musculoskeletal system that have been judged to be unnecessary or harmful even according to latest research results are further performed entirely unimpressed. If it would really be better to consider proven treatments of this type more accurately, we would perhaps have to abandon more beloved methods. This possibly entails the whole belief in the power of these empirical sciences on diseases and disorders in the end. But who would actually want to question this power, given the many examples of probation (paradoxical exclusion of alternatives)?

In practice, scientifically validated misconceptions thus have a long persistence. How much easier it is in QM to stick in this paradoxical way to arbitrary processes of scientifically unverifiable assumptions that are included in them? Furthermore, the widespread belief that quality management improves the quality of processes and products has been confirmed in such a way. The concepts of QM were repeated over the years and have proven themselves apparently (finally the data of the key figures show that objectives are achieved). The paradoxical exclusion of alternatives finally takes place in this circular argument:

> "The quality and the improvement of quality can only be determined when it is measured. Quality can be measured only by checking (comparing) the compliance with certain requirements. Compliance with the requirements is therefore quality and quality improvement."

After this, we can only pinpoint quality with the help of comparisons, and when comparisons are made, then this is quality. The comparison (the checking) with the requirements, arbitrarily filled with contents in QM, however, does not make quality measurable. A precondition not given in QM for meaningful quality measurements would be that these requirements coincided with general quality features and thus with general values. Such a general understanding of quality, which, for instance, is the basis for product comparison in acknowledged product testing organizations,[31] is not given in QM, nor fancied or desired.

2.6. Loss of knowledge through the faith in controllability

Knowledge is getting lost in procedural differentiations that lack meaning. Knowledge is getting lost because we stick to these meaningless processes. Knowledge disappears at the same rate through progress and standstill, through movement and regress, through change and non-change. Knowledge cannot be captured in less than 30 letters, which can even be reduced in computer language to two symbols, to "yes" and "no", to 1 and 0, to current flows and current non-flows. To be or not to be – in the end we are left with nothing more than a paradoxical dilemma. Knowledge appears and disappears like in a spider web that is difficult to grab; it is always reality and illusion at the same time.

Philosophy and religion searched for various places for the merging of these contradictions, for a solution of these seemingly paradoxical images. Often such a place has been described within the individual itself. Knowledge is bound to its carriers and with these to their time and their circumstances. Words only transform into knowledge by the meaning that people give them.[32] It is therefore useless, as in QM, to collect and store abstract knowledge and conserve it with the belief in gain of power and dominance.

---

[31] The measurement problem II is in such an orientation on general values not excluded, but it is still reduced significantly (see chapter IV, section 3.6).

[32] Also the above mentioned science theorist Karl Popper had this conviction. His falsifications were not to achieve their final validity through further experimentations, but through agreements of the people that are part of the respective scientific expert society. Final conclusions of a science to be taken seriously are thus for Popper always results of social processes – in spite of his postulate of falsifications.

The "human factor" is supposed to get a new and less significant role in QM – regardless of all announcements to the contrary. The QM handbooks are meant to store knowledge that is independent of the meaning that its carriers gave it. Exchangeability and controllability – this seems to work for operations with simple structures. Complexity, however, cannot be managed like this. In the process of dealing with knowledge, people are more than a passive factor: they are always creators themselves, developers, or also destroyers. Even though the differentiated process descriptions in QM may have lost their quality, they still give way for linguistic change, for manipulations and influences of any kind. The human factor thus remains unpredictable and cannot be switched off.

The attempt to make employees, deliverers and clients controllable through over-differentiated process descriptions is doomed to failure from the beginning. Companies that are under the spell of QM abstain from the implicit knowledge of the actors. The rejection of this determining knowledge has to be paid for with ever worse product quality, with meaningless management procedures and finally the loss of profit.

3. How QM worsens the quality of products and services

3.1. Declining quality as a result of measurement, process and zero-defect problems

The constantly growing number of quality labels, inspection stickers and trademarks could be interpreted as an indication that today's products and services have become increasingly better. Hardly a product is found on the market without a label that announces: "This product contains carefully measured quality!" But are these announcements by marketing experts really justified? If employees in QM are demotivated, knowledge is decreasing and the controlling influence of management is reduced to a mere juggling with numbers, then of course product quality is also affected. The assumption that the quality of products and services improved under these circumstances seems rather presumptuous.

But the important question is whether the improvement of product quality is a relevant target of QM at all. It was already shown that the very term "quality" in QM should not be confused with a general understanding of quality. The same applies for the achievement of the quality objectives. QM quality objectives relate primarily to financial profit opportunities that are to be implemented by the appropriate changes and savings in the organizational processes. The quality of the products *can* also be improved through these processes, but this is generally not an explicitly desired goal.

In the most influential QM systems, "quality objectives" are predominantly the measurability of the set goals instead of the improvement of the product quality. Only that which is countable and measurable within very short periods – preferably daily or weekly – is relevant. But measurability is a problematic issue. The measurement problems I to III lead to products that lack important or even *the* most important elements, and to products that are, moreover, even flawed.

The process problem then ensures that the so-deteriorated product quality within the organization remains unnoticed. For in carefully differentiated production and work processes, the responsibility for the end result is broken into almost invisibly small portions. Final inspections can always only re-measure a few aspects. In complex processes such as administrative or teaching activities and in the field of all other services such control is even less meaningful.

Finally, the zero-defect problem ensures that really almost all the errors that have been incorporated into the products and the services remain permanently. By firmly committing to targets that were useful at a particular time and under certain circumstances, we waste the opportunity to make easy adjustments to new circumstances and correct errors in a simple way. "Customer orientation", a popular buzzword in QM, is interpreted and implemented in its very own way. Similar to the concept of quality itself, also the redefinition of customer orientation in QM includes pretty much exactly the opposite of what the end users hope for. The following examples illustrate only a small section of the possibilities in QM to deteriorate the product quality in a sustainable and permanent way.

3.2. Declining quality due to measurements

Of course, the quality of work decreases if the one who is to perform the work is busy with something else. When a train conductor counts the stations and trees passed, he is less sure to match the speed of his train with the line and the timetable. If a baker always recounts how many rolls he has baked, he is less able to ensure that, for example, the ingredients' relations and temperature settings are always correct.

Generally, though, such small distractions in work processes do not lead to any big problems. But the situation is quite different in QM. Here the employees are bound to a myriad of such activities that are not part of the actual work process. Measuring and counting their work actions is therefore just as important as the work itself. In the first section of this chapter, it was shown that the reasons that medical professionals give for emigration are not about general work overload and poor pay but just these eternal counts and documentations. For nursing staff, the situation is even more problematic.

Example: Care services

In nursing, for years we have already sacrificed quality resulting from QM measures. Victims are in addition to the elderly and disabled people also the nurses. The time consumed by documentation now involves a majority of the time that should have been used for care. Nurses must not only provide accurate assessments of care needs, but are also obliged to pursue care objectives that are to be achieved by means of a carefully differentiated set of measures. In addition to general nursing documentation obligations in this regard, all the required activities that might be added in the course of care are to be well documented in order to also serve as a basis for further care planning later. A nurse can thus be required to fill out alone for one patient 10 to 20 forms, each with up to 200 criteria. According to estimates of care facilities, nurses require at least 1½ hours of their daily working time on record-keeping tasks.

The high-maintenance patients, however, not only lose almost 20% of their care hours, but are also degraded through the collection of survey criteria. For example, a box should be checked for the criterion whether the patient "repeatedly asks the same questions" (a stressed-out nurse will ignore that she does not always respond), whether the patient "curses" (who wanted to blame him or her under these circumstances?), or whether the patient is even "ready to report complaints" (this patient should be kept an eye on!); under these circumstances, all data protection limits get obviously completely out of sight.

Now one might think that all these so carefully differentiated collected data would improve the care situation of those affected. Since problems do seem to be particularly easy to solve, once we know exactly to the smallest detail what they look like. Nevertheless, this assumption cannot be confirmed here. It is an open secret that in nursing the reduction of staff and staff qualifications are on the agenda. Also consider the bait being thrown for the nursing staff in the implementation period of QM measures: "Only when everything is being documented carefully, you can see what you really fulfil, what quality your work has, which competence it necessitates!" This statement weighs heavily on the affected and today's increasingly poorly paid staff.

The nursing documentation does not serve the patients and the nurses but rather another purpose. Similar to the whole field of medical care, it is today primarily about legal protection. Since if the risk of errors and deficient care services are today increasingly crucial, then at least, nobody should be made responsible for this. A family member may ask why the grandmother was not carefully laid despite the known susceptibility to pressure sores. Some boxes in the right papers checked by the nurses may save us here from many a problem. The documentation thus makes up documents valid in court.

3.3. Declining quality due to defective measurements

The measuring problem III illustrates how product quality may decrease by means of simple false measurements, the measurement situation itself, and finally the defective processing of the data thus obtained. At each stage of a production process measurement errors are possible. Since these false measurements are the basis for further processing and elaboration, they also determine the quality of the final products significantly.

In particular, "products" that themselves are complex – such as services or as in the following example the "knowledge of students" – are often already rated incorrectly in the process of standardization and topped with nonsensical ratios. The additional false measurements result from the fact that mainly subjective (non-objectifiable) estimates are the basis of the measurement. For the end customer – policyholders, banking customers, patients and students – the potential benefit of several services is getting lost in many ways.

The following example – the measurement of the capacity and knowledge of students – will only describe "simple false measurement". The description of the problem could be extended if, for example, in addition, the subsequent processing of the data by the school authorities would be considered.

Example: Student evaluations

Nowadays, teachers are required to maintain differentiated assessment forms that go far beyond the previous evaluation criteria. In some primary schools, there are alone for the categories labour and social behaviour 14 and more criteria per student, which in turn are differentiated in an average of five sub-criteria. In addition, there are performance criteria for each individual subject.

Let us suppose eight such criteria for the following calculation. A specialist subject teacher with two subjects thus has to take into account around 100 (sub-)criteria per student in a class. With 30 students that makes about 2,700 evaluations in only two subjects! The ratings are expected to be updated continuously.

The first problem with such differentiated surveys is created by the survey criteria themselves, of course. The question which criteria should be collected, and especially their respective weights (measuring problem II), can divide teacher colleagues into opponents. The second problem concerns the inaccuracy of such surveys (measuring problem III). It is already obvious that due to the large number of students and the few hours that every teacher spends per week in a classroom cannot lead to any "right" assessment. Silent students in particular usually do not perform in such a way that the criteria of the teachers' forms capture them. In their cases, teachers can often only guess. This means that in the end many mistakes permeate the evaluations. The issue of student ratings has been described in a number of scientific studies on the practice of regular marking. Apparently, arbitrariness and inaccuracy do not only arise for the already mentioned reasons but also due to gender-specific and class-specific prejudices. This problem is intensified with the new additional assessments.

The "differentiated" evaluations, however, do not only remain on the teachers' lists. They are also discussed with other teachers, in order to insure their "rightness". They are included in their assessments and begin to take on a life of their own. This eventually leads to motivation – or in today's schools with QM rather to demotivation of the students. It has long been known that student evaluations quickly evolve into self-fulfilling prophecies. They are not only relevant for the assessment of past performance, but at the same time, they determine the possibilities of the future school career of children. How will the inevitable misjudgements thus act on the "end product", the knowledge and the performance of students? In particular, the students that have been evaluated as underperforming through such carefully differentiated misjudgements will also tend to be weak in performance in the future. Too bad that against this background, the teacher capacities for "promoting and demanding" are reduced more and more. They are not only limited by the fact that teachers are almost completely occupied with the continuous measuring, testing, comparing and documenting. While there used to be additional hours for support measures, they now cease to exist in many places as a result of austerity measures (QM must also be financed).

3.4. Declining quality of the products through "continuous improvement" of the processes

Using QM does not aim at constantly improving the products but the processes in which these products are manufactured or provided. Process improvement is first and foremost the reduction of process costs. Almost everyone has already experienced the consequences of such a "continuous improvement" of products and services of all kinds.

When, for example, engineers have once again "improved" the packaging process, it is impressive to see how even minimal savings in the packaging of each product results in actual amounts considering the production quantities. At the same time, the difficulty of actually getting hold of the product after the purchase has increased for the consumers. The already stressed-out new parents, for example, can often only get diapers out of their plastic bag with the help of scissors, nerves and a lot of patience. Also music and film lovers first have to win the fight with plastic wrap and holding devices of the discs before enjoying the art. "Continuous improvements" that reduce the quality of products and services are, of course, also facilitated by all other savings in the QM manufacturing process.

Example: Services in telecommunication companies

Younger people may not believe that there were times when customers could actually call up telephone companies and reach a service person. Today, it is customary to choose so-called service numbers for problems with telephone and Internet, and dialling these, initially activates a computerized voice. The customer is then asked to clarify his concerns: "as a new customer, press 1, for information on your line, press 2, for questions related to your bills, press 3, for technical questions, press 4, etc..." But what to do when our concerns cannot be properly classified, such as when a new customer has technical questions? Fast decision-making – that will be regretted just a few minutes later or turns out to be wrong – is then necessary.

If pressing a button and the (formerly unusual) perseverance in waiting queues finally leads to the event of the connection with a real person, the anger of most customers is already gone. In the state of desperate gratitude they try to recall the reason of their call, since it already seems like being on the phone for ages. The customers attempt to formulate their request according to the expectations and needs. Now there is the theoretical possibility that the call centre staff can answer the question. The other (by far more likely) possibility is the regret of the service person and the customer is referred to another colleague who is responsible for the specific problem. Before the customer can respond to this, he or she is already transferred to the next service person. Of course, not directly, again, patience is necessary for another waiting loop. Since call transfers do not always work out in call centres, the game is often already coming to an end at this point. Then there are the sounds of farewell in the line, or before that, the obliging voice that is duly grateful for your call but regretfully notes that all lines are occupied, unfortunately. Who has not experienced this?

We can easily imagine how "process optimization" through continuous improvement is achieved in such call centres. First, the customers are separated according to their status (new or existing customer) and their possible requests are differentiated in all details. The necessary staff skills are then also set to address these requests. In QM it is indeed important that the processes are optimized, so that a qualified technician does not have to answer a simple question. After all, an accomplished technician costs the company much more than a short-term trained jobber. The problems then arise from the fact that on the one hand, employees are placed in the best differentiation, but the customers, on the other, cannot be "continuously improved" in this simple way. So the customers with a low need for advice maybe reached the highly skilled technician, while unfortunately the most demanding customers are connected to the inexperienced employees. Due to the failure of the technical routing, which eventually affects all parties, the so-called improved processes can then lead to a premature but welcome end.

3.5. Declining quality due to the exploiting of limits

For the next variant of the deterioration of quality, we return to P.B. Crosby (1980). He clarified unequivocally that quality in QM does not mean "excellence or luxuriousness" but merely the "compliance with the requirements". In QM "compliance with the requirements" means that nothing is delivered that is not included in the operationalized require-ments. The requirements of the key figures encourage manipulation of every kind. Not only can employees contribute to the deterioration of the quality of goods and services by giving priority treatment to the relevant performance indicators. It is usually the stated goal of QM-managed organizations to eradicate any "dissipation". Dissi-pation is here not about the generous distribution of additional services. Waste is everything that is not considered urgently necessary, just anything that is not compatible with the specified performance indicators.

For example, under EU eco-regulation it is sufficient that only a portion of the feed in cattle breeding comes from organic farming. Convinced organic farmers may yet like to fully bio-feed. For most large-scale producers who today deliver organic meat to supermarkets, however, it is dissi-pation to use 100% organic feed. In the end, conventional feed production is much cheaper. The attention to many such small limit exploitations make up a large part of the profit. The problem, of course, applies equally to conventional food production in which legal requirements must be adhered to. It is exacerbated when, for example, limits are exploited by mixing contaminated and uncontaminated food. Product testers often complain about contamination of all kinds. Another artful way to lower product quality in accordance with the standards is to follow the regulations for listed substances determined by the legislature or by external quality auditors, but also add problematic, cost-reducing substances and processes that are not on the lists yet. It was thus found that the contamination of vegetables with specific (test-related) problematic pesticides has decreased, but the use of other chemicals has increased so much that overall contamination still has risen.

Also in the service sector, quality can be reduced arbitrarily with the variable handling of the quality indicators. For example, the allocation of funds for training for the unemployed is bound to the fact that the educational institution has a predetermined number of teaching capacities with specified minimum qualifications. A nationally active education institution then proceeds along these lines. It provides appropriate professionals for the time of application for funds – only to have them released as soon as possible after the approval and replace them by less expensive teachers. The actual quality of the teaching of the so-called quality-managed classes is an open secret to the unfortunate students and their future employers.

The exploitation of limits applies as well for industrial production. In this manner, the product quality of technical equipment, of vehicles, of everyday goods of any kind, is deteriorated again in QM-managed companies. Money will be saved via material, workmanship, warranty and service, where the rival business does not offer anything better. And once the quality is permanently pulled down to a low level, this level will in the course of time (in which all have forgotten that it can be done better) inevitably be taken as the "standard". And then, in turn, certain tolerances of this standard are allowed, whose exploitation must also not be wasted. This generates a spiral of never-ending quality deterioration.

3.6. Declining quality due to further manipulation in the run-up to measurements

The exploitation of limit values in QM is only one way to manipulate the results. It is an open secret that large discounters instruct their suppliers to adapt their products to the test criteria of test magazines.[33] Preferably those products are put on the shelves that have received and keep the "good" or "very good" rating. In addition to the limit exploitation of contamination, it is also common that products only contain the minimum percentages of the expected ingredients. For test results, for example, it may be irrelevant whether the nut content of a nougat cream makes up 20% or 40%. The good colour plays a role in the test – but the additive that produces this good colour does not count. This is also the reason why untreated orange juice, for instance, did not score in a test. Since the testers often do not have the financial and technical conditions to verify the effects claimed for the products, effectiveness checks are also clipped out from the tests. Thus, a skin cream can get a "very good" rating without even verifying one of its promised effects. And finally, they can snag a lot of positive feedback scores if only the declaration of ingredients is complete – regardless of what is declared there.

These small but effective interventions are possible at any point of the differentiation processes (see chapter II, section 4.4). Not only the service "product test" can be manipulated and deteriorated with the help of QM. The artificial reduction of possible errors (see chapter III, section 2), the appropriate measuring time and a little active influence on the so-called "facts" by using "data cleansing" are other ways to finally bring about the quality results in such a way that the access to badges, seals and other benefits are significantly facilitated:

----

[33] This was explained candidly by the chief editor of the German journal *Ökotest* (Ecotest), Jürgen Stellpflug, in the ZDF German television broadcast of Johannes B. Kerner on 16/04/2009.

When American universities send their elaborately designed promotional brochures to as many high school graduates as possible, then this is not done because they lack applicants. Only a high number of applicants for the few existing places guarantees a low acceptance rate, which is in turn a quality criterion for university rankings.

The employees of sub-contractors of a worldwide operating manufacturer of plastic products have to leave the company premises as soon as possible in the event of injury and fake the place of their work accident, since the company has devised zero-defect processes in the security area that must not be called into question by occurring accidents. The quality award for special security would otherwise be seriously jeopardized.

In our quality-managed health care system, many people are getting sicker. This is not because their health changed in any way – but instead, only the new billing procedures by which insurances with many seriously ill receive compensation from other insurances with less severely ill ensure that the diagnoses worsen. A health insurance in Lower Saxony paid doctors for the "correct" diagnosis and a Bavarian Medical Association called on its members to have the 80 lucrative diseases particularly in view when making diagnoses.

3.7. Declining quality due to fixed zero-defect requirements

In QM the leeway in decision-making of the employees should be restricted with the help of dissection of the work processes. Employees are to be committed to compliance with all standards. Processes can thus be completely controlled and steered from above. In earlier times, "work according to the rules" was feared by employers as a means of industrial action that could bring all the wheels to a standstill. Today's official service instructions determine steps so differentiated that the enforcement of a service according to regulations does not come as a threat but as the corporate objective.

It is still impossible to prevent inconsistencies and errors. Hence, it may happen that employees get into real trouble if they want to resolve such errors quickly and efficiently on their own. It becomes particularly problematic when the differentiated requirements, such as in the following example, relate to work processes that are characterized by complexity and a special kind of professionalism.

Example: Medical supplies

There are only very few other areas of science with such large uncertainties and accordingly so frequently changing fads as there are in medicine. In section 2.5 of this chapter, we have seen how almost everything can be proved or refuted with the help of empirical research. In addition, in almost no other field of research, it is so common to consciously fake results. The close connection between the pharmaceutical industry and research contributes the rest to the quality of medical knowledge.

Again and again medications and surgical procedures prove to make mistakes that not only expose people to new suffering, but also often lead to death. So hundreds of thousands of women in menopause swallowed hormones that have been shown to be carcinogenic. Furthermore, the taking of a painkiller substance prescribed world-wide (in Germany sold under the name Vioxx) was blamed for the death of pain-stricken people. Through the surgical treatment of hip joints with the aid of a computer (so-called Robodoc), patients have been permanently damaged, etc. etc... (cf. Blech 2005, Bartens 2008a).

Obvious errors in medicine are for several reasons only taken seriously after many years. On the one hand, some pharmaceutical companies like to profit even from problematic drugs. On the other, the people's confidence in medical procedures is gained through almost religious rituals and demonstrations of respect that are on the agenda when dealing with the "gods in white", through steep hierarchies in hospitals and through successes propagated in the media.

But what happens when this knowledge area "medicine" is subjected to QM? An area that does not only feed its credibility from secured professional competence, but also with the often understandably existential fears of the patients. It is then not sufficient to only measure the patient data, to collect and compare in professional discussions. All this action is used in QM at the end only with one goal: to develop detailed instructions for an "error-free" prevention and treatment.

In recent years, so-called "evidence-based medicine" has gained importance in this context. Treatment recommend-ations for individual diseases are then no longer only regarded as possible treatment methods but also defined as (quality) guidelines. However, we do not only have the problem that the majority of the results of evidence-based medicine are influenced by the pharmaceutical industry (Bartens 2008b: 146) – but that measurement problems I-III cannot be avoided here either, and that real quality is more than only maintaining the standardized treatment regimens.

An over-differentiated approach lead by problematic interests can especially be a disaster for people who suffer from more than one disease, such as the chronically ill and elderly. These patients, who are not at all a small fringe group but rather make up the majority of patients, would then receive different drugs in substantial quantities according to the guidelines for each of their diseases. A fatal effect is here primarily the fact that generally only very little is known about the interaction of different drugs. Fixed pathways in such a knowledge no-man's land harms patients.

It seems that under the regime of QM the health of the patients is less the goal. Furthermore, the guidelines are not first and foremost applied to secure the patient's treatment at the "cutting edge". The main issue in QM-managed facilities is to avoid possible legal consequences from patient complaints. All diagnostic procedures and treatments are to be performed so that the greatest possible legal certainty for the clinic is assured. For the patients, these result in a situation where they will be deprived from obtaining treatments that are not included in these standardized treatment plans. What is generally even more problematic is that the patients are often subjected to treatments that they do not want. A patient may be informed that this or that organ is to be opened or punctured for more accurate diagnosis, and that for treatment reasons again scalpel, radiation and drugs of all kinds have to be applied. Patients who prefer to wait – for a number of diseases, this method has proven to be as effective or ineffective as all the medical procedures – or patients who want other treatment methods are now more than ever regarded as troublemakers.

In fact, the treatment methods are largely determined. Even doctors who would like to go other ways due to their experience and expertise have little chance of change. If something happens, they may eventually be held liable. In order to keep their legal security, physicians have to pay the price to possibly not use individual treatments – treatments that do not accord with the official standards and QM requirements – or to do so only in a narrow frame.

Medical skills such as empathy, holistic perception of the patient, careful attention and especially long-term experience – simply all the virtues that qualified a doctor a few decades ago – are of no primary concern any longer. These skills used to be a good, stable counterweight to the medical "expertise" that is burdened with many problems. The price for the standardized "medical products" is paid mainly by the patients: those patients who get involved in the recommended procedures against their wishes and the hesitation of their doctor as well as those who go other ways, while today more than ever before they have to do without good medical support.

3.8. Declining quality due to wrong priorities

The problem that the most important element is no longer ensured has frequently its effects especially on QM. We have seen how in QM in its typical differentiation processes the essential is simply forgotten or left behind, often unintentionally. In planning (also in the planning of process descriptions) the danger is always present that obvious problems are foregrounded and overstated. Absurdly, the most important element is forgotten precisely because until then it used to "function" and because it had the status of a matter of course.

You can see how the essentials would become lost today if tomatoes no longer tasted like tomatoes, apples like apples, or when technical products had a wealth of features that could only be used by a fraction of customers – if proven products are disimproved. Then the essential is often never to be seen again. Also the here-discussed examples of quality deterioration in hospitals, schools and universities show how the most important element, the holistic view on patients and students are sacrificed in QM with the help of decompositions and splitting hairs, with differentiated "analyses" and instructions.

The following example shows how not only the consumers, but also companies themselves become the victims of QM. The purchase of the product "risk management" may prove a sham in the following way.

Example: The product "risk management"

In order to be prepared for all eventualities, it is common today in modern enterprises to do risk management. All possible risks related to a project are carefully collected, analysed and evaluated. Unfortunately, however, it is a common characteristic of risks that they are unpredictable and that they cannot be assessed in all their scope. They like to appear suddenly, where and when no one has expected them.

The measurement problem II thus plays a prominent role in risk management. The "most important issue" will know to escape a differentiated analysis. Instead, in a risk management system they capture what can be simply detected. By always being focussed on this obviously tangible, the most important element gets more and more out of sight. With each differentiation step the unimportant is becoming increasingly important. The folders and tables created for this purpose, the developed analyses, standards and metrics impress simply through their presence. With each differentiation step the unimportant is not only duplicated. The number of possible errors and conscious manipulations also increases with each of these decomposition steps (see chapter II, section 4.4). Thus, finally errors and risks are minimized that never were any.

In addition, measures to prevent risks tend to represent a risk themselves. This is for example the case if employees are required to stringent checks of their results and then the necessary capacity for the careful conducting of the actual activities lacks. Or if products receive questionable additives in order to minimize the durability risk.

However, a differentiated risk management system does not only generally focus on the least important issue and even becomes a risk in itself quite often, actually leading to being careless. If for example, in nuclear power plants cooling systems fail, the necessary countermeasures are often not activated or done so too late due to other safety precautions. With the sense of having "managed risk" there are often deliberately taken risks. With the help of a "well thought through" risk spreading many a fund manager wasted the money of the customers due to incalculable risk.

The risk-minimizing in management is always very busy with the exact control of circumstances that rather turn out to be trivia in the course of time. For processing the dangers that threaten the company directly and immediately, the employed risk minimizer lacks time and money, motivation and energy. The intrinsic knowledge of the true risks (thus the "right business instinct") that previous generations of managers were demanded as a key competence, is not only unnecessary in addition to risk management today but it is also entirely undesirable.

While the housing crisis in Germany in late summer of 2007 lead – despite existing warnings – to the ruin of investors and to great losses of banks, their "risk management" was obviously only busy with itself.

3.9. Declining quality due to the redefinition of traditional terms

The possibilities for redefining product characteristics such as durable, stable, natural, healthy, rejuvenating, safe, economical, fast, tasteful, functional, innovative in a new way are, of course, also used in QM. In the end, these terms are all adjectives that are always relative by their nature (see measurement problem I in section 2.1). The "stability" of a piece of furniture can, for example, be measured in years or in centuries. The description of the "naturalness" of food can be based on the type and number of contained or lacking breeding processes and genetic modifications, on the degree of processing or the proportion of additives and procedures.

The arbitrariness of the attribution of features is only a first step that can mean that the semantic content of a concept is eventually turned into its opposite. In this way, the putting of central concepts into new words has assumed alarming proportions in QM. In the context of QM processes, not only the concepts of quality and customer orientation experienced redefinitions that do not leave much of the former meaning. In chapter III we have shown what is today understood by zero-error processes and in section 3.11 of this chapter, how the concept of autonomy at universities in Germany has been turned into its opposite. The same applies to the concept of value [34], which in QM does not have much to do with a

---

[34] see Table 1 in chapter I

culturally specific orientation line for the generally recognized and desirable, but is only measured in monetary terms in Euros and cents.

The concept of sustainability underwent a number of semantic changes that often result in exactly that which sustainability should avoid in the original sense. Redefinitions were made here, for example, in the following steps:

- According to the United Nations, sustainability is to ensure the prosperity of current generations without compromising the welfare of future generations.
- The prosperity of future generations is thought of in this context as depending on economic growth.[35]
- Economic growth requires that limited resources of all kinds are not unnecessarily "wasted".
- In order not to waste limited natural resources (labour, raw materials, land and nature), they are to be "exploited" usefully, thus as "sustainable" as possible.

The following describes another variant with which the term "sustainability" can be turned into its opposite.

Example: The product "sustainable investment"

Investors who invest their assets in sustainable investments often assume to no longer be involved in the exploitation of nature and man with their money. Nevertheless, it may happen that in their portfolio there are nuclear industry shares, or of chemical and genetic engineering corporations. How did these shares get in there? A good quarter of all sustainable investment products are not defined according to a positive

---

[35] "We need a new era of growth, an equally strong as socially and environmentally sound growth." This is a key statement on sustainability in the famous Brundtland Report of the World Commission on Environment and Ethics of 1987.

list that sets certain minimum standards, or after a negative list that formulates the specific exclusion criteria, but according to the "best-in-class principle".

According to the best-in-class principle, which is partly the basis of the Dow Jones Sustainability Index (DJSI),[36] those corporations from an industry that provide a particularly transparent report on their social and environmental policies are selected. Whether these reports eventually lead to real improvements in environmental protection or to socially and ethically more acceptable manufacturing processes and products, is often not included in the evaluation. Moreover, the conversion of parts of a company to pre-defined sustainability issues can cause it to get to the top on the list in corresponding ratings – even though the vast divisions are still operating in conventional ways.

The need for sustainable investments grows. With the help of the various redefinitions of the term "sustainability" it can be operated in any possible way today.

3.10. Declining quality due to certification processes and internal and external audits

Certification procedures and audits aim at the inspection of organizational processes by internal and external auditors. These checks take place at larger intervals compared with the usually simple measurements. Like other measurements, these inspection procedures base on previously known and

---

[36] Reto Ringger, the inventor of the DJSI and one of the world's most important representatives of relevant investments, argues about "sustainability" in a dispute: "You are betrayed by a basic, but unfortunately very common misconception. And this is: 'Sustainability has primarily to do with ethics or good and evil.' But these are two completely different things. We see sustainability as an economic dimension that provides enormous potential for investors." (Quote from an article by Willenbrock 2008).

chosen criteria. Thus all can work on these tests and prepare in such a way that they finally receive good results.

What do such evaluations tell us in the end? The result of a single, already announced inspection cannot be interpreted as the rule or as if it were repeatable at any time. Just as such an inspection demands extensive preparation time – in which the required performance is not yet supplied – it is followed by a time of necessary relaxation when the required performance is no longer supplied.

One hour under examination conditions thus "costs" many hours of inferior quality. One consulting process by an insurance seller considered to be "error-free" according to the required criteria is followed by various consulting sessions that do not reach the quality of the inspection situation. In school inspections they scatter sand into the auditors' eyes by lessons demonstrated exemplarily. In industrial production these certification hours and audits receive special attention that is left aside in the usual performance: "The air was out. After we had had enough to do to outwit the certifiers, we mainly had to take care of the orders. Then something always changes, the construction, the material, the tools. Nobody has the time to view and adapt the constantly changing requirements in the manual. These are various folders!"[37] Regular work challenges are augmented by the continuous inspections of useful and – with the increasing degree of differentiation more prevailing – useless requirements. The balancing of the thereby bossed-around employees to the regular audits and certification procedures is by nature reduced performance and – whenever possible – also refusal of performance.

---

[37] A quality responsible cited after Moldaschl (2001: 119, our translation).

3.11. Increasingly declining quality due to benchmarking,[38] ratings,[39] and rankings[40]

With the onset of the financial crisis in Germany in 2007, the true quality of the services of the so-called "rating agencies" became apparent – agencies whose mispricing was not only related to investment funds but also to the creditworthiness of organizations. It is also thought-provoking if in the same year in a rating for sustainability, innovative companies from the organic industry, producers using alternative energy and ecologically oriented financial and insurance industries are hardly listed. Large companies from the chemical industry, though, get the best ranking.

In QM benchmarking, ratings and rankings ostensibly serve the comparison of products and processes according to certain criteria. The aim of this comparison is meant to be the prominence of powerful and cost-effective variants of a feature. In QM, in the end the relationship of costs and profit should be optimized: as much profit as possible at the lowest necessary cost. Through standardization and the logic of performance indicators, both the costs and the benefits are to be packaged into practically manageable parcels. But the quadrangularity of these neat parcels belies the underlying complexity (see chapter III, section 2). By comparing the performance indicators that result from such simplified logic, we obtain the basis for the typical downward spiral in QM.

Agriculture is a good example of an economic sector in which dumping prices took on lives of their own and led to the fact that for many years there was produced more and more with less and less costs. But at what "price"? An exclusive orientation on the cheapest variant inevitably reduces the quality. In agriculture, the declining quality is

---

[38] Benchmarking is the comparative analysis after a previously determined criterion.

[39] In a "rating", products, services and whole organizations are evaluated.

[40] In a "ranking" the previously given evaluations are placed in an order on how they ranked.

caused by an increasing industrialization and related to monocultures, to genetic modification, the increase of fertilizers and pesticides, to factory farms, to exhaustive application of medications, etc. A similar situation can be reported of the food industry, the clothing and the cosmetics industry. Excessive toxins and pollution levels at the same time with not reached conventional quality features do hardly cause any scandals any more. Customers have also long become accustomed to the reduced quality of services. Especially savings in personnel costs due to "quality offensives" have corresponding consequences in the service sector. Qualified professionalism and dedicated motivation are ranked and rated out everywhere where no short-term economic benefits are expected from these employees' virtues (example: comparison of medical practices with the "personal expense ratio" in section 4.6).

If apples are compared to apples, detergents to detergents, and bicycles to bicycles, the problems of comparability can be passed over. The more complex the "products" are, however, the harder it is to see any sense in such comparisons. This problem is exacerbated by the fact that data in benchmarking processes, in rankings and ratings tend to be beautified and thus useless. If companies, administrations and educational institutions aim at cutting their costs to reach the "best" values under these false premises, a further performance loss is programmed.

The comparison of highly differentiated services in banks and insurance companies, in hospitals and educational institutions thus raises the question for suitable standards – what could be the subject of such comparisons at all. While today universities, for example, valiantly seek differentiated answers to this question, the crucial decisions have already been made by an entirely different side. So it has become popular to expose universities and also increasingly, schools to the public with the aid of ratings and rankings. The following example shows in which way the "product school and student knowledge" is affected.

Example: Education and Pisa study

The Pisa studies have not only led to the situation – as described above – that teachers are today more concerned with examinations, the creation of statistics and their own training than with the task of teaching their students. The opportunities to challenge the students' minds a little are also lower since that necessary space for their own development (e.g., by eliminating an entire school year in German grammar schools) has been systematically and thoroughly cut in favour of Pisa query-oriented learning. Every "free" idea is thus nothing but "waste" according to the new quality standards. But a trained bear cannot yet dance. Therefore, today many worried parents believe they have to put fire under their children's feet. The number of coaching schools and students moving in that direction has exploded. Every news agent offers parents' guides, and the market for supplementary learning materials experienced triple-digit growth rates. Under these circumstances the presumption that the improvement of Pisa requested performances relates to improvement of the school system is simply bold. The price for the achievement of dubious standards is high. The price is not only paid with the nerves of children, teachers and parents, private coaching, specific materials and tons of wasted time of everyone involved. Pisa now dictates from outside what our children are supposed to know. The most important – the most crucial element – has been taken from us with the Pisa glasses on our nose. In the land of poets and thinkers, today thinking matters very little – and poetry, does not count at all.

But also the measurement problem III, the faulty measurement, is becoming out of view when considering rankings, tables and point comparisons. It seems to be only of interest to those who have just become victims of such measurements. Accordingly, in the 2006 Pisa study, of all the countries, Norway, Denmark and Sweden, who met showcase functions due to their positive reviews in previous years, suffered bad losses. While on the one hand the responsible persons puzzled about the factual circumstances (less qualified teachers, too little emphasis on the sciences ...), the local population offered a much simpler explanation. The good performance in the previous tests and the subsequent pilgrimages to their schools have always been mistrusted by the Scandinavians, who generally do not consider themselves blessed by education. So now the Pisa-training courses must take place elsewhere.

The presumption of false measurements in Pisa studies does not only relate to the data collection methods (e.g., selection of students,[41] of test questions, of scaling methods and dubious participation motivation incentives[42]). It is also underpinned by comparable studies, which lead to different results. With respect to equal opportunities the Pisa study of 2006, for example, certifies improvement, while other studies, such as the IGLU study carried out in primary schools, asserts that the existing social inequalities have increased.

Example: Rating of the final examination results

When in Lower Saxony in 2006 for the first time a ranking of schools was created as part of the general data collection enthusiasm, the joy was of course great for the top finishers. The sole criterion of this ranking was the average A-level grade! The problem of this ranking with only one measure is obvious: Criteria like the social environment of schools were not considered, such as income and education level of parents, large or small-town milieu, recorded secondary school leavers. Failed students were not included. This led to the grotesque situation that ten poor but passed A-level results hurt the average grade of a school more than ten failures.

---

[41] In some countries, migrant children or students with dyslexia or dyscalculia were excluded from the tests. Similarly, the sex ratio was often not properly considered, or the participation rates were too low.
[42] American students, for example, were given money for their participation.

Forcing schools into competition like this not only ends up costing the validity of the grades and motivation of teachers and students. The price of this public comparison is the distraction from all that is really important: the course contents, the teaching quality and the possibilities of individual student support. The damage may be extended if, as well as public attention or even financial support are subjected to such a ranking, as in the following example of universities.

Example: University rankings

At this point we are not addressing the problems of forming weighting criteria in university rankings and the survey methods that are today not only commissioned by magazines, but also from administration political side. These problems could no doubt easily fill books.[43] Here we are only interested in the question of what are the results of such publications. Will universities accept these "analyses" as an opportunity for general improvements?

In the past years, universities have become "independent" in the course of QM measures. The new "autonomy" involved a drastic restriction of academic self-government, for example through the establishment of new governing bodies. The academic freedom was further curtailed in the context of these "independence processes" by the cuts in government funding. Universities are therefore existentially dependent on a pettifogging making of points in ratings and rankings. Under the new power relations, they "improve" especially according to the requested benchmarking criteria. If the quality of teaching, for example, is rated significantly via the sheer number of publications in a likewise "ranked" list of journals, then you will seek to increase this number, whatever the cost may be. This is not possible without making compromises

---

[43] A small clue to this problem can be obtained when, e.g., transferring the manipulation possibilities in QM described in section 3.6 to the complexity of university structures.

elsewhere. Not merely an inevitable deterioration of the publications is to be expected (the fact that there is a publication is finally more important than what it contains). The capacity for scientific cooperation in other areas, for students training, research and development must be restricted.

Of course, the new standards by which quality is easily measured today, how it is counted and weighted, also allow a much more accurate differentiation between good and bad departments.[44] In particular, in the humanities it is usually difficult to gain points and so the thinking at many universities is more and more "rated out".

Then there is finally not much in the way to show not only top ranking places. A little adjustment to the big show running, an at least rhetorically effective breaking of the "pillarization" of research structures by a few throwaway "excellence clusters" (this is the name of what formerly used to be simply called "cooperation") and you have got the overall elite concept. The vast majority of universities have not achieved the "excellence predicate" from the Science Council or German Research Foundation in this elite competition forced upon them by federal and state governments.[45] Nonetheless, some of them can appreciate this kind of honour, which for many decades could not be achieved because of the historically conditioned, bitter off-flavour of the elitism involved.

---

[44] Today already about 5% to 20% of university funds are distributed according to the new performance criteria. The German government in Berlin even proposed in July 2009 to bind two-thirds of the funds for earmarked universities to "performance indicators", "success fees" and "bounties". The particular advantage of this method is ultimately that only the basic arithmetic operations are requested from the politicians for control of universities and "unruly" professors.

[45] Fellow students of the Journalist Academy of the Konrad Adenauer Foundation have gathered quite refreshing facts on this topic on their website *Geistesspitzen*: http://www.eliteakademie.de/nachrichten-leser/geistesspitzen-elite-unis-in-muenchen-auf-dem-pruefstand.html.

The bond of funds to questionable rankings and excellence initiatives makes it worth to join in and jump on the bandwagons of science. However, will the "elite" that is fabricated on such bases withstand the real challenges of our time that usually show up without any badges or insignias?

4. How quality management reduces value and profit and causes an explosion in costs

Despite all the problems in QM it is often still suspected: "This is all well and good, but at least costs are reduced and benefits are gained when using the QM method." This assumption is probably the most momentous mistake that companies and administrations make. When complex work processes are enhanced with equally complex control processes, then both one and the other have to be financed. The wide gap between on the one hand the QM rhetoric for cost savings ("We do not make mistakes anymore and if we do everything right, we make profits") and the operational cost-reality on the other is expressed in many different ways.

4.1. Quality turns into figure skeletons – harbingers of conceptual and financial losses

Already the quality managers of the first hour were confronted with the observation that the costs for the procedures do not relate to the profits. These argued that the existing business standards can only measure the costs of QM. The advantages – the possible gains that would be caused by QM – are not measurable micro-economically. Instead of a micro-economic game of numbers, the quality of the products should speak for themselves. Evidence of the quality should be provided from corresponding customer surveys. Customer satisfaction, it is assumed, is also the key to economic success. Unfortunately, the quality professionals of the first hour did not stick to this position. In order to increase the acceptance of their actions on the management level, they tried more and more to adapt to a short-term business management logic. "Quality engineers show the effort to link the less legitimate technique (quality management) in a social field (of a corporation) with a more legitimate technique (profitability calculations) in such a way that the less legitimized complies its criteria with those of the more legitimate technique. By subordination to the dominant and accepted technique, the new technique develops a serving character, and thus it gains legitimacy" (Walgenbach 2001: 14, our translation).

The "quality movement" thus took subordination to the business as its mission. Nevertheless, the question remained of how this readiness to subordinate would be presented effectively in practice. Every accountant knows what incredible amount of flexibility and variability the numbers allow. The attempts to adjust QM to the world of business numbers cost and still cost the quality managers not only a high degree of self-denial but also their skills and creativity.

The problem of spurious accuracy in QM is mainly caused by this denial and adaptation processes. The goal of real quality improvement was abandoned. Instead, now they wanted to make measurable what seemed somehow measurable. For this purpose, the depth of the differentiation process analysis was again increased.

In the previous chapters we have already seen which problems always arise. Especially the (unintentional) possibilities of error and the (intentional) "analysis" manipulations increase. The sight of the essential – that often knows to escape measurement – is getting lost. At the end remain dead measurement figures and ratios that promise to make visible at once the potential profit in combination with other figures as "hard number facts".

With this step, the over-fitting to a purely economical, and as every economy student knows, to a large extent also manipulatable and artificial "logic", the claim of actual quality improvements was abandoned. Instead, they fabricated today's figure skeletons in a Frankenstein way; figures that now scare not only employees and managers as ghosts. They take on – with the help of benchmarking processes – a life of their own, which often goes far beyond the boundaries of the places of their creation.

4.2. How QM thinks it saves money

It sounds usually very demanding. There should be a link to the company's visions, circular rule models of quality and models of cost-savings (QkE).[46] However, looking at the scope of QM systems, the details with which the standardization processes are described, the accuracy with which a QM manual is written, the duration of working group meetings where such a manual is devised, and finally the education measures have become necessary so that employees also perform these meetings correctly. Well, if you look at all this, you may expect with good reason that the cost savings in QM must be developed in the most complicated manner.

But in principle it is always the same way, how costs ought to be saved in QM. As a matter of attunement the missions and visions of the company are considered in order to determine the objectives of a particular department, which are as ambitious as possible. Subsequently, the given process structures are to be recorded and fixed. Certain employees, often the supervisor, receive the new title "process owner". Similarly, the boundaries to other departments of the company are redefined and now called "interface definitions". The most important step in the definition of process structures is the definition of key performance indicators and parameters. Everything obviously countable and measurable is written down and forms either a figure on its own or it is processed together with other countable and measurable figures. For example, in industrial production you can measure how many pieces are produced per employee. In hospitals you can count how many appendices are removed every six months. In administrations you can measure how many kilograms of paper per department are needed every week.

---

[46] QkE is the abbreviation of German "Qualitätskosten-Ersparnis-Modell" (quality cost savings model, cf. Simon and Janzen 2001).

The actual cost savings are now meant to come about by subsequently controlling the actual parameter values – for example, the actual number of products produced per hour. Such values are then collected over a certain period of time. You can then compare them with the corresponding actual values in other similar departments or with those from other, similar companies. If in such benchmarking it is now determined that other departments of the company or other companies reach better actual values, then QM offers a particularly effective solution to address this issue: The target states of the measured values are changed! So it can, for example, be specified as the destination that the number of products produced per hour is increased or that the paper consumption per week is reduced. Even though the competition may not be any better, this "method" is meant to further enhance performance. In QM, this performance increase is then called "continuous improvement".

The basic idea of the cost savings in quality management is therefore neither new nor in any way complex. It is neither bothered by visions nor by any missions. It is neither a "model" nor a "method". Cost savings in quality management means first of all, that the measured actual values are either increased (number per time unit, patients per hour, sales per customer) or decreased (product quality, consumption of energy and time).

4.3. "Analyses" of costs and benefits in QM

The recorded "quality costs" include, in addition to the costs of error prevention (the actual QM costs), also the costs of testing procedures (testing costs) and the subsequent costs of errors (error costs). Testing costs include, for example, end and acceptance testing of products but also quality assessments and laboratory tests. Error costs are incurred, for example, for scrap and rework, impairment, goodwill and compensation cases. The advantage from the perspective of QM advocates of the joint consideration of all quality costs, is that the QM costs occur only as part of all quality costs. The disadvantage, however, is that in the business logic costs should always be reduced.

Therefore, the costs of QM are treated separately, in a new delimitation to the testing and error costs. Finally, it is argued, it makes a difference whether a method prevents errors (such as QM) or, as in the second case, already occurring errors must be corrected. If there were less or no errors, less or no refinishing was necessary. Following this view, they make a distinction between the "costs of compliance" and the "costs of deviation". The costs of compliance include all those costs that ensure compliance with the quality requirements – in particular, all expenses for the QM. The costs of deviation cover all those costs that must be incurred to correct the existing errors and deviations.

According to this new weighting, the costs of compliance – the actual costs for QM – appear, of course, all the more justified when the costs of deviation rises. In cost-benefit analyses for QM, they developed a lot of imaginative ways to raise costs for deviations immeasurably. Especially those "errors" contained in the deviations create an inexhaustible field for the origination of costs. Now there are, for example, operations defined as "errors" that were previously seen as natural elements in a work process. Any activity not included in the process descriptions is then not only superfluous but a contribution to the "costs of deviation". This holds for the patient, customer or client dialogue that exceed the time set-point, or for an error prevention measure that has not been explicitly defined in advance.

Unfortunately, such strange interpretations of the term "error" are in QM far from just being "theoretical". In the production of a company, for example, workers were instructed to simply refrain from the corrections in their work area. Errors that are only caused in other departments – no matter if large or small – should be left to those departments themselves. Also in cases where, for example, unclear details need to be clarified before signing the contract, since this may be rated as an "error" from a quality perspective (ambiguity does not exist anymore). It is then estimated how often this "error" occurs in a given period and how long it takes to complete its processing. The index can then be called "clarify equivocal process details in hours per half year". Then, a precise calculation of the cost of errors is carried out as follows:

> "Clarify equivocal process details in hours per half year" multiplied by the hourly wage: 180 hrs/half year multiplied by € 75 = € 13,500 per half year."[47]

In connection with such calculations, the actual costs of errors of this type would even be much higher, because the customers could be scared off by such errors. These error costs are then called "strategic error costs" or "external error costs", and they would rise the more, in our example, the more unclear process details were clarified before the conclusion of a contract. In this manner, the costs of deviation rise continuously. In the course of a QM procedure, it is possible to reduce error costs that did not exist at the beginning, before inserting the QM measures!

While the costs of the deviation are getting higher and higher in horror scenarios of the above type, of course, the potential benefits and profit opportunities that arise by QM have to be highlighted in an adequate clarity. The benefit opportunities in QM are to be found in the "error prevention" and in the "continuous improvement".

The potential benefits resulting from the error prevention and error reduction are derived from the error costs. In the above example, the error costs are € 13,500. The "unclear details" that were identified as significant cause of errors, are now resolved and the employees are instructed accordingly.

---

[47] Now it is not at all the case that such "calculations" are conceived only by quality managers. This fanciful example to the deplorable "costs of deviation" is found in a written "definitive work" by university professors.

In conclusion it is generously estimated by what percentage the value of the indicator "clarify equivocal process details in hours per half year" is improved by this method. Let us start from an in QM quite usual 50% improvement estimate, which is confirmed by the employees fearing for their jobs. These 50% are then calculated by around 80% as actual savings. Finally in our example, we could reach saving possibilities of approximately € 5,400 (€ 13,500 by 0.50 by 0.80) by preventing errors that don't really exist!

In a similarly adventurous way, the potential benefits that result from all other processes of a "continuous improvement" are calculated. The value changes of the corresponding figures often move in dizzying heights of up to 80%. The explanations of such estimates are likely to be omitted. The usual euphoria for detail and measure in QM does not seem to capture the estimation of these figures. The absence of detailed information is then justified with the argument that the real potential for improvement of the measures taken were in reality still much bigger. Evidence of the success of such "continuous improvement" is then, for example, the "fact" stated that with reduced staff numbers customer satisfaction has increased. Who would still want to point out that the employees work to their limits and only maintain operations with quality loss after such thorough calculations? And who would still be interested in the scientific knowledge that customer satisfaction increases all the more often measured due to the appropriate adaption of the measuring instrument?

The QM costs seem to justify themselves in these methods.[48] The question is if the so-calculated benefits are at all reflected in profits or whether the "improvements" worsen the service and product quality to such an extent that the competitiveness of the company is at risk. This question, however, can only be answered indirectly and in the distant future. The so-constructed figures should speak for

---

[48] In the organizational sciences literature this is often referred to as "Potemkin quality villages".

themselves, while the fluctuating and buttery soft ground on which they stand is forgotten.

4.4. Costs that are ignored in the cost-benefit analyses of QM

If they are at all performed, then the analyses of costs and benefits usually in QM only include the obvious additional costs that arise from the QM training, the newly hired QM staff, QM systems, external consultants, audits and certifications. This often ignores the most significant costs completely. This means that the employees' time incurred for training, working group meetings and especially for the extensive documentation tasks does usually not form part of these calculations. It is probably implicitly assumed that employees are already paid and can thus be engaged in a self-financing manner. This assumption is quite presumptuous if you take into account the actual staff time that is consumed in the QM procedures. Nor is the staff time that is not directly but indirectly consumed included in the cost-benefit calculations. Such indirect wastes of time in control and change processes are not only the anxieties and fears of employees. They especially consist of the employees' activities (of avoidance and obviation) and considerations in dealing with the new measures. Another often neglected aspect of costs concerns the need for additional information-processing software and hardware and corresponding IT staff. In the end, all the collected data must be processed and stored.

While in the economy the private sector at least sometimes bothers to perform cost-benefit analyses of QM, this does not apply to the public sector, schools or universities. There is generally no desire to know about the costs associated with the control of complex processes through equally complex QM methods. Obviously the responsible persons realize that QM method expenses will far exceed potential savings into the foreseeable future. If in the course of QM measures jobs are axed, then the unanswered question remains of what of the previously given service quality is left over. But since the bill is paid by taxpayers and contributors who are not entitled to an answer on the cost-benefit question, an end of the QM enthusiasm in government and in education is not yet in sight.

4.5. The dreamed of cost savings – and the reality

At first glance, it is apparent that the seemingly new but in fact old basic model of cost savings, which is also used in QM, shows at best short-term effects – effects that quickly reach their natural limits. Even if employees are increasingly put under QM thumbscrews and raw materials and semi-finished products are saved in areas where the competition has nothing better to offer, both methods cannot be extended endlessly. Even if a doctor who treats 50 patients daily may be forced by "quality measures" to take care of 80, then there will not be any real scope beyond this. A car is produced cheaper today by the QM method of replacing metal with plastic parts, but even here there are natural limits.

The possibilities to change the relevant objectives in such a way that costs are really saved are always limited. What is however not limited in QM are the possibilities of measurement. The measurement problem I (see section 2) makes clear that the possibilities of measuring can be extended endlessly through imagination and creativity. Measuring is the comparing of comparisons that are compared with each other. Measuring is not without reason the favourite activity of a dedicated quality manager. Measurement processes do not necessarily end in usefully optimized process descriptions or plausible profitability calculations.

Thus, in QM not only the actual costs but also the product and production quality are measured out forever from these processes. We have seen what performance indicators can inflict on private companies and public administrations. Not only do products and services deteriorate steadily under the regime of QM – for when employees turn the tables and only fulfil what has to be fulfilled according to the figure requirements, the consequences are devastating.

Problem measurements and corresponding problem key figures in the complex social processes of the quality are the rule of the day. In chapters II and III it was shown that the root causes for this failure lie in a differentiation of the process analyses that is too deep: incorporation of errors and deliberate manipulations are unavoidable. These errors are cemented in the further course of the quality process using detailed process measures to guarantee a permanent adherence to absurdities. Not even creative and smart managers and employees can save much then.

The benchmarking makes the craziness of the situation finally completely solid. The competition will keep the actually interesting comparable data secret as long as possible and beautify it to suit their agenda.[49] Finally, if data are available for benchmarking, the question arises of what is really being compared. When measured information of one organization is compared to that of another, then these are usually different things. In the following examples in this chapter we will demonstrate that the benchmarking game not only proves to be nonsense with respect to irrelevant figures, but that it also fails in relation to determining the "adjusting screws" of QM.

If after completion of the quality measures we get a figure report, which suggests cost reductions and profit increase, we should therefore look at it carefully. The alleged profits by QM-level measures can generally not be assigned, but they have to be dreamed of arduously. Where today real savings are noted, it is mostly on the account of better know-how of employees who do not get discouraged despite all and of further developments in (information) technology. These are

---

[49] Even public institutions are not afraid to prepare data accordingly. The fact that federal and state ministerial departments adjust and beautify statistical statements on, e.g., poverty, unemployment and state debts, often raises sad attention.

thus circumstances that are taken by QM, but have nothing to do with it.

While on the one hand cost savings and gains can only be predicted, suspected, or hoped for vaguely, on the other the actual costs show their impact immediately. There are the initial costs for the training of quality supervisors, quality managers and internal quality auditors, the costs of setting up whole "quality assurance" departments, the costs of employee trainings, the costs of audits and certifications, etc. And since we are dealing with "continuous improvement", these certifications have only very limited validity. The costs' spiral will thus soon start all over again. In addition, there are the previously described costs that are usually ignored in QM: costs of management and employee involvement, the costs of the time loss caused by the working group meetings and required surveys, the costs of additional information technology, etc.

In QM, the employees are supposed to be controlled in their work processes as completely as possible. So in addition to the costs for the introduction of QM systems, we have to consider the costs for the permanently rendered external and self-checks (which are usually not included in the calculations of QM). Employees do not only have to list their labour services in detailed checklists. Also the respective superiors are obliged to continuously monitor and evaluate the work performance of their subordinates in differentiated ways. Through this QM pampers and cares for a bureaucratic hydrocephalus that would even look modest compared to the former East German planned economy.

In connection with the on-going costs of control in QM, the general administrative expenses, of course, also increase. Not only the quality manual ought to be prepared and constantly updated. We have to create the cross-company background capacities in order to record and process the results of the continuous measuring, weighing and counting. Finally, the available data incites to ever new "analyses" and change processes. The technology development in recent decades may absorb the huge costs that are associated with this to some extent. But in some areas where QM is applied, these costs explode without any possibilities for compensation. Especially in the services sector, in schools and in hospitals, the employees require a substantial part of their working capacity for documenting activities (rather than for the execution of such activities). It is not surprising that the naive fallacies of QM have their impact especially in these areas. Because unlike in the industrial and technical fields, the QM measures are often taken very seriously and implemented meticulously by all those involved in this area. Due to the lack of compensation possibilities of costs by technological progress, the economic loss caused by QM is far larger than in industrial private companies.

As described in the previous chapters, cost problems in the public and private sector do not only arise by the introduction and maintenance of the QM system itself. The other QM consequences – that is, mainly the reduction of employees' motivation, the steady loss of knowledge, the increasing reduction of management to mere controlling and ultimately the steady decline in product quality, provide a clue to the actual dimensions of the QM total cost.

4.6. Examples of cost issues

Example: Comparison of domestic and foreign production with the figures "average personnel costs", "personnel costs per produced unit", "personnel costs of the sales price", etc.

For many medium-sized industrial enterprises (SMEs), it is tempting in view of the comparison of wage costs to relocate their production abroad. If the conditions in the selected country in terms of further indicators, such as for infrastructure, personnel qualification and raw materials supply give a good impression, the decision seems simple. Thus, about 5% of all jobs have been moved to a location abroad in recent years.

Nevertheless, many companies had to learn painfully that "low wages" are only one side of the coin, and they have since moved their production back home.[50] What they underestimated in the shift abroad are the costs of communication problems that are usually not only of linguistic but also of cultural nature. They usually underestimate the additional costs for the transport of goods and transport damage as well, and costs for additional quality control, for the dealing with taxes, general legal and import issues and the widespread bribe payments in many countries where wages are low. The figures for infrastructure usually prove to be in practice only one side of the coin. Low energy costs, for example, can be very expensive if the supply system often fails and then the cheap employees are forced to inactivity, as is often the case in developing countries.

But what is especially underestimated – and this does not only hold for the SMEs – are the losses that derive from knowledge and patent theft. "We have people trained there,

---

[50] According to a report by Blank and Wirtz-Nentwig in the German television program *plusminus* (ZDF), 17/10/2006.

how to develop systems and how to process them. The so highly-qualified employees then migrated, partially built their own business or even went to competing companies – and they took the know-how with them," complained an SME manager, who back-shifted the production from Poland to Germany (Blank and Wirtz-Nentwig 2006). Another businessperson made similar experiences: "They very well tried to produce this key technology on their own, and I have been plundered from the highest level. The production we raised was only deceit to gain my trust" (ibid.) Instead of getting hold of a dominant position in the low-wage country, their own home sites are put at risk from self-initiated competition.

Example: Comparison of administrations with the figure "total work time per case"

In the course of administrative reforms and needs for savings in the public sector, QM has also found its way into this area. The indicator "total work time per case", for example, is an attempt to find out where work is comparatively more effective and where not, and where options for job cuts based on this figure exist. The question is, however, how the relevant data can be collected and, above all, what the relevant data are at all.

Administrative professionals usually know what problems are associated with the figure "total work time/time per case", and therefore they prefer to stay away from it. Instead they oblige outsiders with generally less knowledge for quality tasks in the public services, such as management consultants of different qualifications. But since here also money is to be saved, it is possible that the task to figure out where and how staff can be reduced is transferred to a trainee. This actually happened in a small community, where a student of Public Business Economics, who – still in the first years of his studies – got into such a predicament.

The poor student then tried to find help in an online forum on controlling – otherwise we could not report the case here. In this forum, he was warmly recommended to apply the figure "total work time/time per case". It was not of much use for him, because the office for which this measurement had to be calculated was the Building Administration Office. The student intern complained that he cannot even understand the work processes and also that "almost everything is regulated by law". We can imagine what kind of damage such a "study" will have done for the staff of the Building Administration Office. We can imagine how the employees in turn also obstructed and exposed the innocent intern, who studied their positions with respect to savings, or pitied him at best.

But let us now assume such research would proceed in a little more professional manner than in this sad but unfortunately not extraneous example. Nonetheless, there remain unsolvable problems:

- The complexity of most administrative processes entails that the description of the manageable quantifiable contents (work time, case number, paper consumption...) are opposed to a myriad of hardly measurable contents (expertise and commitment of the staff, quality of citizens' service, quality of the internal processes etc.).
- Administrations – even if the departments have the same name – are often hardly comparable with each other. While in one administration, the social services may administer certain tasks, the same are administered by the health department in another one. Tasks of the human resources department in city A are often coordinated in various, specialized departments within city B, etc.
- QM processes are usually not openly described as processes that should result in savings but as necessary steps to effective quality improvement. Employees who do not feel they are being taken seriously or feel deceived will put all their energy into

avoidance and blocking activities. The basic condition of complexity in administrations opens up unlimited possibilities for them.

- Case numbers can be manipulated. Again, the administrative complexity guarantees that the case numbers can be increased or decreased as desired.

Case numbers in the administrative area do not correspond to what controllers and quality managers desire. The price for such surveys, which are still carried out, is high. It does not only take the time and energy of the employees but also their motivation and commitment. This is usually enduring. The core question, namely: "How can administrative processes be improved and become more efficient?" is pushed into the background bit by bit with every senseless questionnaire.

If the results of such "examinations", however, are taken seriously and actually determine set points for the staff, it usually becomes really expensive. Employees now put their energy rather in the achievement of the standard and measure values than in meaningful case management. This will have consequences for what is simply called a "case". For indeed we are here dealing with – what is mostly forgotten in the whole administrative measure operating – people of flesh and blood, who do not want to be understood as a number or a figure representative.

Costly is mainly the processing of objections and complaints of those citizens who do not want to accept the arbitrariness and inefficiency induced by quality measures. An already overburdened bureaucracy is further blocked by the incapacity to act through quality management. We may therefore raise the question: "Who controls the controller? Who checks the quality of the quality managers?" The German Municipal Community Centre for Administration Management (KGSt)[51] wanted to offer its member

---

[51] KGSt is the abbreviation of German *Kommunale Gemeinschaftsstelle für Verwaltungsmanagement.*.

municipalities special help. This led to the founding of the inter-municipal network IKO in Germany in 1996.[52] The IKO network carries out comparison projects in which municipal services are measured and compared with the help of indicators. But if you are now hoping that these measurement and metrics breathe life into professionally founded research, you are hoping in vain. The IKO network does not want to improve the contents of administrational actions but only the figures that pretend to measure these contents: The IKO network established the target to increase the total customer satisfaction to 90% with a minimum of 30% very satisfied customers (in a survey of 2005 it was 25%) for 2007.[53]

With such noble goals it is understandable that the answer to the question of how, where and what is measured – and above all with whom – at which time under what pleasant conditions is ultimately more important than the solution to content problems. And if finally everything comparable has been compared, if each municipality works according to the measure statistics just like any other – can consistent evaluation become unnecessary all by itself?[54]

Example: Conversion of a research institution in a profit centre company – figure "contribution margin per profit centre"

In order to make a private, medical research institute more profitable, the institution was restructured and individual departments were formed as so-called "profit centres". For each profit centre, they determine the arising variable

---

[52] IKO is the abbreviation of German *Interkommunales Netz*.

[53] And in fact in 2007, a value of 94.2% was achieved! (cf. Korte and Stallmeyer 2006).

[54] This equality has already been achieved in the evaluation of old peoples' and nursing homes – actually any institution is now evaluated as "very good", meanwhile the "personnel costs per nursing home resident" have fallen.

(employment-related) costs, including prorated overheads.[55] Likewise, each centre is attributed a (fictitious) share of the total turnover. The difference between the two sums then results in the contribution margin for this department.

In the initial planning phase, the required times and costs should be allocated exactly to individual research projects in order to make precise offers to the clients later. The corresponding surveys in this context also included the necessary personnel costs, differentiated according to the different qualifications of the staff.

Problems occurred already in this survey phase, because the employee times that were surveyed to be necessary already seemed to make the future projects more expensive to a considerable extent. What was the reason for this? The employees documented their activities very carefully with awareness of the coming changes. They now followed work steps meticulously, which were necessary due to the regulations (health and safety, certain rules for dealing with the test subjects and the test equipment, etc.), but which were generally not fully taken into consideration in regular practice. Insiders also perceived the professional qualifications associated with respective steps as a radical change of the actual conditions. Above all, the times recognized as necessary of highly-paid employees rose.

But the thus increased employee costs were not the only problem. What made the performance of the institute considerably more expensive than before were the new control mechanisms, necessary data collections and processing, which incurred further even after the stocktaking phase. The aim of all measures was meant to be a cost reduction. Thus, the actual data of the analysis were reduced arbitrarily for further planning to a fixed price. On the one hand, this led to considerable problems with the staff, which partially resulted in terminations and thus in a loss of

---

[55] Overheads include, e.g., costs for the management, administration and data processing.

knowledge on the staff level. Due to the hierarchical conditions, the employees of lower levels were, in addition, also affected disproportionately by the cutbacks. They suffered therefore insofar a "double reduction" as their activities were already considered detrimental in the surveys. What impact did the new situation have now? How were the increased costs and the disproportionate cuts on the executive staff level compensated that were caused by these new testing and documentation requirements? The QM insider already knows. The success or the losses of each department that were "made demonstrable" in the above described manner, led to large and small manipulations on all levels of the institution. There were subjects of tests also listed in the statistics of tests where they did not participate. There were results that were made "significant" through any calculations. "The Institute could no longer afford projects that were unsuccessful due to the data collected and that could cost customers," says a former employee. The pressure to succeed became stronger and freedom was limited at all levels. It is this freedom that is generally seen as a prerequisite of innovative research that decides on reputation and name of an institution.

In addition to the research itself, this concept is, of course, subject to imaginative manipulations – especially due to the way the contribution margin of each profit centre was calculated. In particular, the allocation of appropriate monthly turnovers of a single business unit cannot be calculated in a "clean" way. It is also determined by power politics to a considerable extent. For the above example we are left to note that in this institution, the cost issue could not be satisfactorily resolved, despite the introduced measures. In the meantime, other consultants have to deal with the problem.

Example: Comparison of doctor's surgeries with the figure "personnel expense ratio"

A business consultant, funded by the state, advertises to locate "reserves in the doctor's surgery". He takes an example of a surgery as a sign of his knowledge and suggests that a comparatively high figure "personnel expense ratio" (staff costs in relation to total turnover) does not necessarily mean that there is too much staff. He takes the further key figure "monthly turnover per nurse", which in this example has an average value. With this additional figure, he believes to prove the statement that the work efficiency of the team and the organizational structure of the sample surgery are healthy and thus not too many nurses are employed. According to this "analysis", the problem lies in high personnel costs. The consultant thus recommends "adjusting the salary level".

The conclusion that the number of nurses is "just right" if you reach an average monthly turnover per nurse in comparison to other surgeries is far-fetched. Unfortunately, the figure "monthly turnover per nurse" does not mean anything else than the ratio of the monthly turnover of the doctor's surgery to the total number of nurses. The contribution the nurses make to this turnover – and this would be the crucial question here – is completely uncertain. The contribution of nurses does not only vary individually. It may be particularly high in relation to the turnover contribution of the physician – for example, if the nurse is an accounting professional. Or it may be particularly low, for example, if the nurse scares away the patients. In addition to the performance of the physician, though, other circumstances also have an impact on the turnover: the patients' structure (higher monthly turnover with more private patients), the prescription structure, the treatment structure (how long are what treatment methods carried out at what cost conditions), the use of equipment, specializations to specific treatment fields, etc.

But let's suppose that after further measuring and weighing the conclusion could be drawn that all these circumstances "are just like in average compared surgeries". Let's suppose, we are dealing with an average surgery and that we could really believe that the nurses are paid more than the average. The doctor would adjust wages accordingly – that is, reduce them. The surgery consultant now goes to the next surgery and realizes, for example, that the wages are lower there than in comparable surgeries. What would be the consultant's advice? To increase wages? Probably not. The lower wages, though, will now enter into the figure of "average wage per nurse" and reduce the optimal value of this ratio.

In the end, in such quality improvement processes, the whole average cannot remain on average. It has to get inevitably below average! Too bad taxpayers have to participate in such improve-worsening operations that in the end are also harmful to their health. Too bad, especially for the medical surgeons, which seriously rely on such "analyses". Then they have to learn that staff and patients cannot be handled in a way to do justice to the figures. And above all, this holds for the statutory and private health insurances: what is profitable today, is already taken from the catalogue of tomorrow.

References

Adams, Scott. 2003. *Das Dilbert-Prinzip*. München: Redline-Wirtschaft.

ÄrzteZeitung. 2009. Jahresendausgabe, 22/12/2009. Available at:
http://www.aerztezeitung.de/politik_gesellschaft/gp_spec ials/jahresendausgabe-2009/p-8/default.aspx (last access: 15/01/2017)

Bartens, Werner. 2008a. *Vorsicht Vorsorge! Wenn Prävention nutzlos und gefährlich wird*. Frankfurt/Main: Suhrkamp.

Bartens, Werner. 2008b. *Das neue Lexikon der Medizin-Irrtümer: Noch mehr Halbwahrheiten, Vorurteile, fragwürdige Behandlungen*. Frankfurt/Main: Piper.

Batchelor, Stephen. 2002. *Nagarjuna – Verse aus der Mitte: Eine buddhistische Vision des Lebens*. Himberg: Theseus.

Blank, Ingo & Wolfgang Wirtz-Nentwig. 2006. *Abenteuer Ausland: Warum Unternehmer nach Deutschland zurückkehren*. Reportage in ZDF television programme PlusMinus, 17/10/2006. Available at:
http://www.daserste.de/plusminus/beitrag.asp?uid=vikxx mom10j048od&cm.asp (last access 20/11/2006).

Blech, Jörg. 2005. *Heillose Medizin: Fragwürdige Therapien und wie Sie sich davor schützen können*. Frankfurt/Main: Fischer.

Deming, W. Edwards. 1988. *Out of the crisis: quality, productivity, and competitive position*. Cambridge: Cambridge University Press.

Capra, Fritjof. 1999. *The Tao of Physics: An exploration of the parallels between modern physics and eastern mysticism.* 4th edition. Boston, Massachusetts: Shambhala Publications.

Crosby, Philipp B. 1980. *Quality is Free: The art of making quality certain.* New York: Mentor.

Gallup 2015. Pressemitteilung Engagement Index Deutschland 2015 (www.gallup.de). Online document available at: http://www.gallup.de/file/190031/Pressemitteilung%20zum%20Gallup%20Engagement%20Index%202015%20for%20download.pdf (last access: 11/01/2017).

Gausemeier, Jürgen, Alexander Fink & Oliver Schlake. 1995. *Szenario-Management: Plane und Führen mit Szenarien.* München, Wien: Carl Hanser.

Geistesspitzen: Elite-Unis in München auf dem Prüfstand. Available at: http://www.eliteakademie.de/nachrichten-leser/geistesspitzen-elite-unis-in-muenchen-auf-dem-pruefstand.html (last access: 06/01/2017).

Hofstadter 1999. *Gödel, Escher, Bach: An Eternal Golden Braid.* New York: Basic Books.

Hondrich, Ted. 1995. *Wie frei sind wir? Das Determinismus-Problem.* Stuttgart: Reclam.

Kalbfleisch, Dirk; Annette Schellenberg, & Siegfried Gröf. 2001. Wissen braucht Engagement – Wissensmanagementsysteme als Plattform für prozessorientiertes Qualitätsmanagement. *QZ – Qualität und Zuverlässigkeit,* 46 (2), 132-133.

Korte, Rainer & Andra Stallmeyer. 2006. Instrumente anwenden, die man anderen empfiehlt: Steuerung der KGSt-IKO-Netz-Arbeit mit Zielen und Kennzahlen. *Innovative Verwaltung*, 28(1/2), 18-21.

Krämer, Walter. 2000. *So lügt man mit Statistik*. München: Piper.

Luhmann, Niklas. 1984. *Soziale Systeme: Grundriß einer allgemeinen Theorie*. Frankfurt/Main: Suhrkamp.

Maier, Corinne. 2006. *Die Entdeckung der Faulheit: Die Entdeckung der Faulheit. Von der Kunst, bei der Arbeit möglichst wenig zu tun*. München: Goldmann.

Martinson, Brian C.; Melissa S. Anderson, & Raymond de Vries. 2005. Commentary: Scientists behaving badly. *Nature* 435, 737-738.

Masaaki Imai. 1998. *Kaizen: Der Schlüssel zum Erfolg der Japaner im Wettbewerb*. München: Ullstein.

Mauthner, Fritz. 1923. Circulus vitiosus. In Fritz Mauthner (ed), *Wörterbuch für Philosophie: - Neue Beiträge zu einer Kritik der Sprache,* Volume 1, 248-250. Leipzig: Wilhelm Braumüller. Permalink: http://www.zeno.org/nid/20006180191 (last access: 06/01/2017).

Moldaschl, Manfred. 2001. Qualität als Spielfeld und Arena: Das mikropolitische Verständnis von Qualitätsma-nagement – und seine Grenzen. In: Harald Wächter & Günther Vedder (eds), *Qualitätsmanagement in Organisationen: DIN ISO 9000 und TQM auf dem Prüfstand*. Wiesbaden: Gabler, 115-138.

Reinker, Susanne. 2007. *Rache am Chef: Die unterschätzte Macht der Mitarbeiter*. Berlin: Econ.

Sainsbury, Richard M. 2009. *Paradoxes*. 3rd edition. Cambridge: Cambridge University Press.

Simon, Thomas; Martina Janzen; Christian Lampe; Werner Prischmann, & Heinz Best. 2001. Einsparen – aber kontinuierlich: Senkung der Qualitätskosten durch Regelkreismodell. *QZ-online* 46 (9), 1171-1173. Available at: http://www.qz-online.de/qz-zeitschrift/archiv/artikel/senkung-von-qualitaetskosten-durch-regelkreismodell-einsparen--aber-kontinuierlich-343171.html (last access: 10/09/2014).

Taleb, Nassim Nicholas. 2007. *Der schwarze Schwan: Die Macht höchst unwahrscheinlicher Ereignisse*. München: Hanser.

Walgenbach, Peter. 2001. Historisch-institutionalistische Analyse der QM-Entwicklung. In: Harald Wächter & Günther Vedder (eds), *Qualitätsmanagement in Organisationen: DIN ISO 9000 und TQM auf dem Prüfstand*. Wiesbaden: Gabler, 3-25.

Warzecha, Bettina. 2004. *Organisationale Planungstheorie*. Wiesbaden: Deutscher Universitätsverlag.

Wehrli, Ursus. 2002. *Kunst aufräumen*. Zürich: Kein & Aber.

Weick, Karl E. 1985. *Der Prozeß des Organisierens*. Frankfurt/Main: Suhrkamp.

Willenbrock, Harald. 2008. Wir stehen bei der Nachhaltigkeit erst ganz am Anfang. – Finden Sie? Für Investmentmanager gibt es doch nichts Schöneres als Alkohol, Tabak und Pornographie. Interview with Reto Ringger and Hedrich Werner. *Brand eins*, Year 10, issue 12, 40-45. Available at: http://www.brandeins.de/archiv/2008/glueck/wir-stehen-bei-der-nachhaltigkeit-erst-ganz-am-anfang-finden-sie-fuer-investmentmanager-gibt-es-doch-nichts-schoeneres-als-alkohol-tabak-pornografie.html (last access: 06/01/2017)

.

www.ingramcontent.com/pod-product-compliance
Lightning Source LLC
Chambersburg PA
CBHW031811190326
41518CB00006B/292